IN THE TIME OF MADMEN

MARK A. PRELAS

ISBN 9789493276178 (ebook)

ISBN 9789493276154 (paperback)

ISBN 9789493276161 (hardcover)

Publisher: Amsterdam Publishers, The Netherlands

info@amsterdampublishers.com

In the Time of Madmen is part of the series Holocaust Survivor True Stories WWII

Disclaimer. The events portrayed in this book are based on stories told to me by my parents and family about their lives before my birth as well as my own personal experiences. While the events are true to best of my memory, some of the names and identifying details have been changed to protect the privacy of people. In some cases, multiple characters have been compressed into a single entity. It is not possible to recall a conversation word for word, but the dialog is representative of the context.

CONTENTS

FOREWORD

Never judge a book by its cover, my mom always said. Never judge a person by how they look, by their accent, or by their religion. Impressions formed only by sight and sound are false and do not reveal a person's character or the depth of their soul. Those who judged my mom by these shallow standards as a new immigrant to America never had the pleasure of knowing her and never recognized the underlying strength of her character nor the cavernous depth of her soul. As a young woman, she had talent and ambition. She was a world-class swimmer at a young age. She understood and spoke many languages. Her goal was to become a doctor and help people. But, like many of her era, the Great Depression and the apocalyptic Second World War curtailed her dreams. Life became a struggle for survival. She was one of the many who performed *Zwangsarbeit,* which means "forced labor" in German. During the Third Reich, over 12 million foreign concentration camp prisoners, prisoners of war, and foreign civilian workers were abducted and exploited to serve as slave labor for the German war machine. Like many other young women of that time, my mother would never have the chance to pursue her aspirations. It is in life-and-death struggles where heroes are born and strength of character shines. In this, she was a beacon. She led a simple life and touched many through her passion for helping others in need. She made America a better place. Like other courageous people, she never sought nor desired adulation. She was content. I see facets of her in immigrants I have known.

Katicà Bek, circa 1947

In memory of Katicà Bek on the occasion of her 100th birthday.

I kept my promise.

INTRODUCTION

Each of us has personal heroes and villains. In my life, I have known both. Every family has wonderful stories to tell about a heroic ancestor. Mine is about my mom, Katicà Bek. She Americanized her name to Katheryn when she arrived at Ellis Island, New York, in 1952, as one of the many displaced persons who arrived from Europe after World War II. But you can't understand her tale without knowing where she came from.

Mom's tenacity was derived from her family. She was part of the lineage descended from the great Matija Gubec. He was the leader of the Croatian-Slovene Peasant Revolt from January 28 to February 8 of 1573. Gubec was a serf who worked on the estate of Baron Ferenc Tahy. Known for his oratory and organizational skills, Gubec was chosen by the serfs as the leader of their quest for basic human rights. Gubec's army of 10,000 poorly armed serfs suffered defeat at the Battle of Stubičko Polje at the hands of a well-armed force of 6,000 led by Tahy. After his capture, Gubec was taken to Zagreb, where he was viciously tortured and executed. Yugoslavia honored Gubec by erecting a statue of him in Podsused-Vrapče. Mom's stubbornness, even in the face of a hopeless situation, must have had its roots in Gubec.

Mom's parents were relentless in providing for their family during some of the most terrifying times in human history. Her father, Marko Bek, was born in 1885 to a Jewish family. Josip, his father, had married Jela Mihak, his mother, in 1884. But before Marko turned ten, his father died. Jela was alone and desperate. Her widower cousin, whose name has been lost in the fading memories of surviving relatives, had always admired Jela. He married Jela and became Marko's stepfather. There are fairy tales about evil stepparents. For most people, stepparents do not turn out badly. In Marko's case, the fairy tale was a reality. His stepfather was a true villain. He beat Marko and forced him to sleep in the barn with the cows. He refused to provide food to another man's son and Marko had to live off what he could scavenge and what Jela slipped to him under the threat of a beating by her husband. She eventually had children with her cousin. After the birth of his half-siblings, Marko's life must have seemed hopeless. Jela had little time for him because the babies needed her.

At 14, Marko ran away. He learned and developed the skills necessary to survive on his own, both in cities and the countryside. Marko wandered to wherever he could find work, a meal, and a place to sleep. He worked as a farmhand and discovered that he excelled at the nuances of agriculture and animal husbandry. By the time Marko turned 18, he already stood six feet eight inches tall and was handsome. He had a thick, manly mustache. My mom's fondest memory of my grandfather was his perfect white teeth. He was proud that he went through life without ever having a toothache.

In 1905, Marko took a job with Franjo Ilinic, a farmer and the mayor of the village Popovača. It was then that he first met 13-year-old Jana Ilinic. Jana was the daughter of Franjo and Mara, whose maiden name was Furet. Jana's beauty and intelligence impressed Marko. Franjo was a good man, charismatic, and a devout Roman Catholic. His wife, Mara, was a convert to Catholicism from Judaism. Mara's family had disowned her after she converted, so I know little about them. Franjo and Mara treated Marko like he was part of the family. Marko came to think of Franjo as his mentor and father figure.

Marko started going to church with the Ilinic family and he converted to Catholicism. It paved the way for his budding courtship of Jana. On February 4, 1911, Marko and Jana married. Their son Alojz was born on February 15, 1912.

Marko was attuned to his surroundings because of his years of living by his wits on the street. He understood that the instabilities in Europe were growing stronger. He knew conflict was coming to the Balkans before it happened. The first war pitted Serbia, Montenegro, Bulgaria, and Greece against the Ottoman Empire. It started on October 1912. A second war would follow in 1913. The Balkan wars left 200,000 dead but did not settle the underlying issues. These conflicts set the stage for World War I.

Marko decided to move his family to America. He left Jana and Alojz behind with Franjo and Mara until he could earn enough money to send for them. Marko used his savings to travel to Antwerp and bought passage on the steamer *Kroonland,* heading to the United States. Marko arrived at Ellis Island on March 28, 1912. The United States was ripe with opportunity. Marko took a job at the shipyards in Philadelphia. There he learned skills in construction and welding, which served him well for the rest of his life. He saved every penny he could from his salary and sent money to Jana.

He was close to being able to send for his wife and son. Then the Serbian nationalist Gavrilo Princip assassinated the Archduke Franz Ferdinand in Sarajevo on July 28, 1914, which started World War I. Even worse, the epicenter of the war was close to Popovača, a village just southeast of Zagreb. Marko had to return to Popovača. Travel to Europe was almost impossible in the middle of a war. Marko made his way back by finding passage on a freighter going to North Africa. He then worked on various fishing boats going to ports that brought him closer to home. He meandered from one to another until he reached Split, Yugoslavia. From Split, Marko traveled north along the Adriatic coast until he reached Popovača. An interesting circumstance was that he must have come within 30 miles of the family home of one-year-old Jure, my father, who lived in Budimir, just northeast of Split.

With a pocket full of money and few or no options for taking his family along a treacherous path back to the United States, Marko purchased a large tract of land just south of Popovača. He had a keen eye for agriculture; he knew the tillable land was rich and the forested area thick with mature trees for building. There was a source of water with several large ponds and a stream flowing through the property. He started felling trees and began building a home for his family. One last thing that Marko did not know at the time was that his land sat on a major reservoir of oil. By the fall of 1914, Marko completed the house and barn. Jana and Alojz moved in. Then Marko purchased livestock and other necessities to make the farm a first-class operation. For the first time in his life, Marko was happy and content. But fate had other plans. Austria-Hungary was desperate for soldiers, and it forced Marko to serve in the army.

Marko left his family in the care of his father-in-law, Franjo, when he departed. During basic training, the officers noticed Marko for his imposing stature, his intelligence, and his leadership skills. His comrades would follow him anywhere. Marko was the prototype of an emperor's personal guard. After basic training, they sent him to Vienna for advanced instruction to become a member of the emperor's guards. While serving the emperor, he rose through the ranks. They commissioned him as an officer in the guard.

Austria-Hungary had a weaker military than Germany and barely hung on during the first year of the war. The second year of the war became more perilous because the relationship between Italy and Austria-Hungary had deteriorated. Italy joined the allies on May 23, 1915, and declared war on Austria-Hungary. With an additional front to defend, the army was stretched too thin. In the spring of 1916, the emperor was forced to redeploy the bulk of his personal guards to the eastern front. Marko's unit was part of the redeployment. On June 4, 1916, the brilliant Russian general Aleksei Brusilov engineered what came to be known as "Brusilov's Breakthrough," an offensive along the southern part of the eastern front that took the Austro-Hungarian troops by surprise. The Russians captured Marko and his men.

Russia sent their Slavic prisoners of war to work on farms on the western side of the Ural Mountains. German and Austrian prisoners of war were sent to Siberia to work in the mines or to northern Siberia to build a railroad. Marko ended up in the north working on the railroad. There was little or no security in Siberia because of the vast distances a prisoner had to travel to escape. That was all that the Russians needed as a deterrence. They treated the prisoners the same as the peasants who labored on the railroad. They were free to live as they wished. The prisoners had little desire to escape because it was enough of a struggle just to survive in the brutal conditions. If you did not live in the railroad camp with everyone else, you died. Marko's intelligence, knack for agriculture, and construction skills allowed him to thrive. He gained the respect of fellow workers and supervisors.

On October 25, 1917, the Russian Revolution erupted. Marko must have thought he would be going home soon, but the revolution grew into a civil war between the communist Red Army and the opposition White Army. The Red Army desperately needed experienced soldiers and recruited among the prisoners of war. Many of the Slavic prisoners chose to join because they felt a kinship to the Russians. In the Austria-Hungary empire, they were oppressed. Even some Germanic prisoners of war joined the Red Army. However, Marko did not. They left him to live in a settlement at the end of the railroad line. Marko was trapped in Siberia long after November 11, 1918, when World War I officially ended. He scratched out a living using his talent as a farmer. The civil war raged from November 1917 until October 1922.

In the meantime, Jana got word in the summer of 1917 that Marko was alive in Siberia. But she hadn't received any letters from him. Jana became more frightened when the Russian Revolution began. Jana was hopeful that the Russians would let their prisoners of war return home. But Marko did not come back. After World War I ended, she anxiously anticipated the homecoming of her husband. However, there was no sign of Marko. She began to despair. Rumors persisted that many of the prisoners were choosing to stay in Russia. There was speculation that some had started new families in Siberia. She worried that Marko might be one of them.

The soldiers who did return from the war brought a terrible disease with them, the 1918 Spanish flu. Even though its name might imply an origin in Spain, the flu was carried by American soldiers from Fort Riley, Kansas, to the western front in late fall 1917. The Spanish flu had already killed 30,000 American soldiers before they reached the shores of France. It then killed an additional 15,000 Americans on the front lines. The flu quickly spread through the ranks of the Allies and then the Axis. When the war ended, the virus had the mobility it needed to spread around the world with the returning soldiers. From the fall of 1918 to the winter of 1919, the second and most terrible wave of the flu spread, causing a devastating pandemic that killed between 40 to 100 million people worldwide. It was horrifying because the young and healthy were most at risk. An infected person with a strong immune system overproduced cytokines which bind to the receptors of cells to promote the proliferation of immune cells. An overabundance of cytokines causes immune cells to attack the healthy cells of the host. This is known as a cytokine storm. Once a healthy cell dies, its fluid enters a person's bloodstream. This fluid buildup fills the lungs and the victims suffocate. The process is rapid. There were accounts of healthy young people leaving for work in the morning feeling fine and, by the afternoon, they suffocated from the effects of a cytokine storm. Jana had heard stories of people dying in the streets of Zagreb and it terrified her. She desperately needed Marko to come home.

In the meantime, Marko was living on the margins in northern Siberia. When my mother was a little girl, Marko told her about his life in Siberia. She particularly remembered his stories about the cold. So, when my sister and I complained about the cold of a wintry day in Colorado, she loved to tell us about the icicles that had formed on our grandfather's mustache during the Siberian winter.

The virus found its way to Siberia. Yet Marko endured and survived. The pandemic ended in the summer of 1919. Marko wanted to leave Siberia, but he knew it was too late in the year to attempt an escape. He still needed more supplies for the journey. Marko resolved to be patient and prepare well. He planned to make the journey during the spring of 1920.

In the winter of 1919, tragedy struck in Popovača. Jana's father died. Without the help of Franjo, Jana could not keep up with the farm. At the end of her rope, she asked Ivan, the older brother of her childhood friend, to help. Ivan was charming, attractive, and had had lingering feelings for Jana since childhood. He was a big man, oozing with confidence. He reminded Jana of Marko. Ivan had failed at farming and business but saw an excellent opportunity. He agreed to help on the farm. Jana was vulnerable. She was depressed about losing her father and had given up hope that Marko was coming back. As the weeks passed, Ivan pursued a romantic relationship. At first, Jana resisted. But then she succumbed by convincing herself that Alojz needed a father and that she needed a man. As the season turned from winter to spring, the affair between Ivan and Jana blossomed. In late April 1919, Jana was pregnant with Ivan's child. In January 1920, Alojz's half-sister, Marie, was born.

In January 1920, the war between the Red Army and the White Army had shifted to the south. This gave Marko the opportunity he had waited for. He had accumulated supplies to make the journey home. Marko began the 3,000-mile trek in late February 1920. With the skills he had learned as a 14-year-old runaway, Marko was adept at riding the rails, foraging for food, and blending in. He found his way out of Russia. The world had transformed in four years, as had the face of eastern Europe. His journey took him through new countries formed after the war, like the Ukrainian People's Republic, Hungary, and Yugoslavia, in which his beloved home Popovača was now situated. In April, as spring was in full flower, Marko arrived at the house that he had built for his family. When Jana saw Marko, her heart filled with joy; then the realization of what she had done struck her. Ivan, who also saw Marko, was furious. He demanded that Marko leave the land that he now claimed as his own. Marko was substantially thinner from his travels and years of poor diet. He was not as formidable looking as Ivan had remembered. Brimming with confidence that he could intimidate Marko, Ivan again ordered him to leave the farm. But Ivan had no inkling of the man he was facing. Marko had legendary strength, stamina, and willpower. The people of Popovača told stories about Marko picking up full-grown men with one hand. As a soldier in the Austro-Hungarian Army, Marko was the most fearsome soldier in his division. Plus, Marko had something to fight for—it was his house, not the house of some interloper who had taken away everything that he held dear. Ivan started the attack and paid a dear price. With broken bones, Ivan fled Popovača, never to be seen again. Marko took back his home and family.

Marko was angry with Jana when he learned about Marie. He felt betrayed by the woman he loved. It was the thought of her that had given him the strength to survive the cold winters of Siberia, to overcome constant hunger, and to maintain the willpower to find his way across 3,000 miles of desolation in the middle of a civil war. Jana was ashamed and frightened by Marko's anger. She gathered up some belongings, Alojz and Marie, and rushed to her mother's house about a mile away, leaving Marko to rage alone.

Left isolated in deep thought for a few days, Marko pondered his future. He knew in his heart that he would forgive Jana but also knew that he could not raise Marie as his own. Perhaps he drew from his own experience as an abused child growing up with a stepfather who hated him. I admired much about him, but I struggle to understand the decision he made. There is a sad realization that no human being is perfect, even though my mother believed her father could do no wrong. We all have the capacity to be heroes or villains. It is part of life and we make the choices which define us. All that one can hope for in the end is that the scale will tip toward being a good person. Marko would not raise Ivan's child.

The people of Popovača were happy to hear about Marko's return after being presumed dead. But the town's euphoria and the gossip soon died down. Marko and Jana talked. Jana initially resisted the demand of returning home without Marie. She considered leaving Marko, but there were conversations with the local priest about preserving the sanctity of marriage. Friends and family also believed that she should go back to Marko without Marie. Jana finally gave in to Marko's wishes.

Marie's fate was unsettled. Ivan's family refused to raise the infant, and Ivan was nowhere to be found. Finally, my great-grandmother, Mara, took Marie in. Marko was satisfied and Jana returned home with Alojz. But the solution created a family rift that would never heal.

The Bek household would never be the same, but life went on. Jana was pregnant by late April with Yelca, who was born in January 1921. Katicà, my mom, came along on November 22, 1921, followed by Inga in March 1924. My mom's youngest sister, Dragica, was born in October 1927; and her baby brother, Pepic, in January 1930.

MOM'S STORY, PART 1

Life on the Bek farm was hectic. There was little time for the underlying hard feelings and resentment about the events related to my grandfather's return to blossom. The world was in the third year of the Great Depression. Farmers did not feel the full impact of the Depression, but it was still painful. Money was scarce and purchasing something not produced on the farm was a luxury. The Bek farm produced enough food for themselves and fed quite a few people in Popovača and Zagreb. The primary means of commerce was barter.

Most of all, four little girls and a baby boy separated by nine years were a challenge for Jana and Marko. Little Katicà was a handful all by herself. She was curious, smart, and headstrong. The word "no" to little Katicà meant to go faster. Marko and Jana seemed to spend most of their time attending to her.

It is important to give more of a sense of the area where they lived. Popovača was comprised of three communities. The Ashkenazi Jewish community spoke Yiddish among themselves, but they could also speak German and Croatian. Popovača also had a large community of ethnic Croatians who were Roman Catholics; they spoke Croatian and German. There was a small community of ethnic Serbians who were Serbian Orthodox, and they spoke Serbo-

Croatian and German. Jana and Marko could speak Hebrew, Yiddish, German, and Croatian, but in the home they spoke only Croatian. This was a rich environment for Katicà, who had an incredible gift for languages and a love of socializing.

Marko's stepbrother, Streete, was a hatter in Popovača. Jela and her husband raised him in the Jewish faith. Streete learned Hebrew, Yiddish, German, and Croatian from his parents. Marko never held the abuse he suffered at the hands of his stepfather against his stepbrothers or stepsisters. His stepfather was cruel to his own children as well. Marko and Streete were close friends. Mom had fond memories of Uncle Streete because he encouraged her gift for languages. He worked with her to perfect speaking Hebrew, Yiddish, and German. Mom cherished growing up in Popovača because she could mingle with the various communities and learn about each of the cultures. When she was five or six, she walked the mile to Popovača alone. My grandparents worried about my free-spirited mom because she would leave without asking them. So many bad things could happen to a stubborn child traveling alone on the road to Popovača. I recall a story that Mom told me. There was a pack of wolves that lived in the woods close to the road between Grandfather's farm and Popovača. Once, a child traveling alone on this stretch of road wandered too close to the woods during the cold winter and the hungry wolves attacked him. I believe my grandparents were most concerned that fear never stopped my mom from doing something dangerous.

In rural Croatia, feuds were a matter of honor and would boil for a lifetime. For my mom's grandmother, Mara, the feud with the Bek family over Marko refusing to raise Marie was a matter of honor. Mom never hesitated to go to Mara's house or any other place where she and the other Bek daughters were not welcome. Mom loved visiting Mara and Marie, even though her parents told her many times not to. One incident that Mom often spoke about was the time she dropped by while Mara was baking a pastry. Mom was ten years old and precocious. She remembered the delicious smell; she was going to stay until Mara had to take out the pastry. My mom asked what was in the oven, but Mara pretended that there was nothing. In her mind, Mom pictured a nice juicy blueberry pie. She wanted to have a piece of that pie. Mara knew what her granddaughter wanted and was not going to give her any. Mara kept up the charade and refused to take the pastry out of the oven as long as Mom was there. The burning smell became stronger. Mom left, disappointed, after the smoke from the ruined pastry filled the air. Mara was pleased that she had won the battle of wills with her stubborn granddaughter. Despite Mara's open hostility toward the Beks, Mom always felt that Mara was secretly happy to see her. Mara would ask about Jana, Alojz, Yelca, Inga, Danica, and Pepic. Talking about them delighted Mom.

My mother's half-sister, Marie, was understandably cold toward the Bek children. Mom never gave up trying to break the ice between them. Marie and the Bek children attended a one-room school. My mother's classmates gravitated toward her. She loved people, loved life, and had a charisma that was almost hypnotic. These were traits that she had in common with her charismatic grandfather, Franjo. Marie had a special place in Mom's heart. She regretted that Jana had abandoned Marie. Marie never embraced my mom, but sometimes she would forget that Katicà was a Bek. Those were the moments that my mom treasured most.

Katicà was an unusually bright child. Miss Marta, the teacher, taught at too slow a pace to keep Mom's attention. Miss Marta often chastised Katicà for fidgeting, making a noise, talking to others, daydreaming, and sleeping. When Katicà was ten, in the early fall just before harvest, she talked to her friends once too often. Mom recalled that Miss Marta lost her temper and used a pointer like a whip to strike her across the forehead. It caused a cut that bled profusely. Katicà jumped up from her chair crying in pain and ran out the door, heading straight for the Bek farm a mile down the road. When she reached the farm, she burst through the kitchen door. Jana jumped. Katicà had blood streaming from a wound on her forehead and her school dress was bloodied. Jana reached for a clean wet rag and held her panicked child, pressing the rag to the wound to stop the bleeding. "It will be all right," she whispered to Katicà. Jana's soft voice and reassurances calmed Katicà. "Miss Marta hit me," she said.

A good deal of what I know about this story comes from talking with my mom and Aunt Inga over the years. The incident was a popular topic of Bek family discussions during the long winter nights on the farm while Mom was growing up. Mom said that her explanation about being hit had shocked her mom, but Jana held back from blurting anything out loud. Jana focused on the wound. She cleaned it and reached for the needle and thread. She was an expert at stitching up the deep cuts that seemed to occur too often on the farm. Resisting the urge to ask questions, Jana focused on the stitching while Katicà sobbed. She decided to sort this mess out later. Jana finished and washed Katicà's forehead with some soap and water. She dabbed on some strong plum brandy called slivovitz to disinfect the area and wrapped Katia's forehead with strips of rag bandages. Jana took Katicà's bloody dress and underwear off, washed her body, and put on her nightgown. Jana could tell that her daughter was in shock but that she did not have a concussion. She gently put Katicà in bed. Fortunately, Danica and Pepic were taking their afternoon naps, and the commotion did not wake them. Jana waited for Yelca and Inga to return. She was resolved to seek answers from them. Katicà drifted into sleep and Jana listened to her rhythmic breathing. Jana and Marko tried hard not to show preferences among their children, but a casual observer could see that Katicà was their favorite. Jana was not one to let her imagination run wild. She held her temper but wondered to herself, *Why in the hell did Marta hit Katicà?*

The afternoon went slowly for Jana. Danica and Pepic woke up from their naps. They drank some milk and spent the rest of the afternoon playing together. Jana watched them but could not stop herself from thinking about Katicà. Finally, Yelca and Inga opened the door. "How is Katicà?" they asked.

"She is sleeping," Jana whispered. "Katicà is fine."

Inga observed, "Katicà's head looks bad."

"She will be all right, Inga," Jana said, sighing, then inquired, "What happened?"

Yelca, the cautious daughter, responded, "I did not see what happened."

Jana looked at Inga. Jana knew she always got in trouble along with Katicà during class. "Katicà was talking and Miss Marta turned around and hit her with her pointer," Inga confessed.

Jana showed no emotion. As was routine every day after school, Jana went to the kitchen table and sliced some bread and cheese for a snack. The children sat down. There was a jug of fresh apple juice that Jana had squeezed in the morning. She poured each child a small cupful. Yelca and Inga were hungry. Danica and Pepic played with their food. They talked, laughed, and ate in good spirits. Jana sat down, deep in thought, waiting for Marko and Alojz to come in from the field. When the children finished, Jana asked Yelca and Inga to take Danica and Pepic to the back bedroom to play. The little ones loved to play with their big sisters. Yelca and Inga could hold Danica's and Pepic's attention for hours. Jana needed them to work their magic today.

Jana was still thinking when she realized it was late and Marko and Alojz were about to come back from the fields. She had not yet prepared supper. Jana thought about what she could make in a hurry. Fortunately, there was some leftover sauerkraut, some cured ham in the smokehouse, bread that she had baked in the morning, fresh churned butter, and goat cheese. There was juice and a bottle of wine to drink. She warmed the sauerkraut and ham. Yelca set the table while Inga watched Danica and Pepic. Jana placed the food on the table while Marko and Alojz were in the barn putting up the animals for the night. Katicà was still asleep, and Jana did not want to wake her. Marko entered the house through the kitchen door. The kitchen was small. Marko could see Katicà in the bed near the kitchen area. He noticed her head was bandaged. "What happened to Katicà?" he asked. Jana signaled for him to follow her into the bedroom at the back of the house. The children could hear Marko's voice rise. They talked for what seemed to be hours to the hungry children, but the discussion actually lasted only ten minutes. Jana came out first and did not stop. She marched out of the kitchen door. Marko called after Jana, "Be careful, it will be dark soon." Jana did not hear him. Jana walked as fast as she could. *Why the hell did this have to happen today?* she thought.

Marko looked at the children and said, "Let's eat." He poured each of the children some juice and some wine for Alojz and himself. Marko glanced over at Katicà to see if she was awake. He had hoped that her beautiful green eyes, which he always teased her about, saying that they looked like the eyes of a cat, would be open. But they were closed. Jana, before leaving, had instructed Marko to let Katicà sleep. When Katicà was ready, she would wake up and eat.

Jana walked at a brisk pace toward the schoolhouse where Marta lived in a back room. She pounded on the door.

"Who is it?" Marta inquired.

"Jana Bek."

Marta had dreaded this inevitable visit most of the day and slowly opened the door.

Jana barely contained her wrath. "Goddamn you," she said. "Don't you ever hit my daughter again!"

Jana's anger shocked Marta. She had never heard her curse before. "Let me explain," she pleaded.

"Never hit my daughter or any of her sisters," Jana interrupted. She paused, which gave Marta the opportunity to give a heartfelt apology.

"I am deeply sorry. I did not mean to hurt Katicà. It was accidental and will never happen again."

"You tell that to Katicà," Jana countered.

"Is she all right? Will she be able to come back to school tomorrow?" Marta asked.

Jana could see in Marta's eyes that she was sorry. Her anger subsided and she replied softly, "If she feels better, I will send her back."

"Katicà is the smartest student I have ever had," Marta responded. "She can do anything that she puts her mind to. I believe she will study at the university someday."

Her response did not surprise Jana. She had observed Katicà's gift after taking her daughters to Venice for a vacation during the summer. Katicà was most interested in initiating conversations in Italian with native speakers. At first, the conversations were awkward, but during each subsequent conversation, Katicà picked up more and more vocabulary and grammar. By the fifth day, she spoke so well that even native speakers thought she was Italian. Jana marveled that when they returned to Yugoslavia through the border crossing at Trieste, Katicà engaged the Italian guards in conversation. The guards did not check Katicà's papers, believing that she was an Italian citizen crossing the border to shop. They checked Jana's, Yelca's, and Inga's papers. Jana watched in amazement as Katicà approached the guards on the Yugoslavian side of the border crossing and again engaged them in conversation. They let her pass because they could tell that she was a Yugoslavian citizen coming back from a vacation. Marko and Jana had often talked about Katicà and her extraordinary intelligence. Marko dreamed that one day his daughter would attend a university to study science, a subject area that he had fantasized about studying if only his biological father had been alive while he was growing up.

Jana responded, "Perhaps you are right. When she feels better, I will send her back to school." She turned and started the long walk back home.

It was dark when Jana returned, and the house was in chaos. Katicà, Inga, and Yelca were giggling near the bed; Danica and Pepic were in the back bedroom asleep; and Marko was sitting at the table. Alojz had already left for his small shack on the other side of the barn, where he lived, to retire for the evening. The dishes were piled up on the table. Jana sighed. She was glad to see Katicà up and back to her old self. There was a lot to do before Jana could go to bed. "Come on, girls, let's clean off the table," Jana ordered. She still needed to prepare dough for tomorrow's dumpling dinner. She had some potato and onions for a stuffing. The plums could not wait another day, so she prepared her famous *knedle s sljivama,* a delicious plum-filled dumpling that my mom would later make for me when I was growing up. It was based on the recipe that Jana had passed to her.

Katicà was up early the next day. Jana could hear her humming. She pulled herself out of bed and Marko woke. It was time to finish making the dumplings and to prepare breakfast. Jana was glad to see that Katicà was happy. "How are you feeling?" she asked.

"I am hungry," Katicà said.

"Would you like some bread and cheese?"

"Yes, please, but can I have some butter too?"

"Of course," Jana answered. She watched as her daughter buttered the bread and said, "I am glad to see you are eating. It will give you strength and you will feel better."

"Yes, Mama," Katicà responded.

"I think you are ready to go back to school."

A look of fear came across Katicà's face and she blurted, "No, Mama. I don't feel well."

"You must go back to school," Jana answered.

"No, Mama," Katicà pleaded.

"Miss Marta said it was an accident, and she is sorry," Jana said as she tried to persuade her headstrong young daughter.

"It was no accident," retorted Katicà.

Jana glared. "I will not argue with you; you will go back to school."

Katicà knew her mom's tones, and this one indicated that there was no room for negotiation. She always tried to obey her parents. "Yes, Mama," she whispered.

Jana watched as Katicà, Yelca, and Inga walked toward the schoolhouse. She wondered if it was too soon to send Katicà back as she lost sight of the children.

Halfway to Popovača, Katicà said sternly to her sisters, "I am not coming."

Yelca and Inga looked puzzled, and Inga asked, "Why not?"

"Miss Marta hit me," Katicà responded. As an afterthought, she added, "Promise me you will not tell Mom."

Both Yelca and Inga tried to persuade their sister to go to school with them, but they knew it was a hopeless argument. When Katicà made up her mind, no one was going to change it. They promised to cover for her.

Katicà watched as her sisters disappeared over the next hill. Their voices gradually faded. Katicà decided to spend the day at the large pond on her father's farm. The pond had plenty of interesting insects, plants, and animals to study. There was a spot where she could watch the animals drink. It was warm, and the sun was out. She walked around the pond and examined the bugs, the plants, the fish, and most of all the frogs. The frogs interested Katicà because they swam so well. She wished she could swim. No one had the time to teach her, even though she had begged her parents to do so. She marveled at the frogs' smooth movements and the speed at which they traveled through the water. There was not a cloud in the sky. She was hot and her stomach growled with hunger. In her school bag, there was a lunch that Jana had packed. Katicà loved the lunches that her mother made. Jana always gave each of her daughters their favorite foods. For Katicà, it was a thick slice of fresh-baked bread with butter, two slices of cheese, a pickle, and some dried fruit. Her thermos flask had fresh milk. She opened the cloth wrapped around her lunch and placed it on the ground with its contents on top. She licked her lips and devoured the bread and butter, her favorite part of the lunch. When she finished, she laid on the ground looking up at the branches of the trees above her and daydreamed. *I know I can swim like a frog,* she thought. Katicà got up, took off her clothes, and waded into the pond. She launched herself forward, and she imitated the frog's stroke. It turned out that Katicà was a natural-born swimmer, and she spent the rest of the afternoon practicing her new skills. When it was time for school to end, she reluctantly got out of the pond to dry off, put her clothes back on, and packed the cloth and the thermos flask into her school bag. She walked to the road and met her sisters. At home, she could think only about the pond and dreamed of swimming.

For the next two weeks, Katicà went to the pond and swam. She had perfected the frog stroke and could glide effortlessly through the water. The season was going to change from fall to winter, and Katicà knew that her glorious time at the pond would soon end. Even though she felt guilty about missing school, she could not give up swimming while the weather was still tolerable.

A couple of weeks later, Jana was in Popovača and happened upon Miss Marta. "Is Katicà feeling better? When do you think she will come back to school?" Marta inquired.

Shock could only describe how Jana felt, but she did not express any outward emotion. She responded, "Soon," and walked away, befuddled.

Jana would not confront Katicà that night. Instead, the next morning, Jana asked Alojz to watch Danica and Pepic and then followed Katicà. Jana wanted to know what she did during the day while missing school. Jana watched her daughter get into the pond and then was dumbfounded as Katicà gracefully glided through the water.

When Katicà got out of the pond to eat lunch, Jana left without confronting her daughter there and then. Jana decided to wait until the evening. In the meantime, Katicà blissfully finished eating and returned to the pond to swim some more.

As Yelca, Inga, and Katicà entered the house, Jana greeted them. "How was your day at school?" Jana slyly asked.

The girls fidgeted and quietly said in unison, "Fine, Mama."

"What did you study, Yelca?" Jana inquired.

"History," she responded.

"What did you study, Inga?"

"I worked on arithmetic," Inga answered.

"How about you, Katicà?" Jana queried.

"Ah, biology," Katicà said.

"Really?" Jana replied. "Tell me more."

Katicà fumbled for a plausible answer and blurted out, "Frogs."

"Oh," said Jana. "Did you chase one around the pond while you were swimming?"

"Um," came out of Katicà's mouth.

"I know where you have been for the last two weeks," Jana said.

Katicà turned red. "I am sorry, Mama."

Katicà was reprimanded and punished that night after Marko returned from the fields.

The next day, she went back to school. She studied harder and mostly never angered Miss Marta again. But her passion for swimming grew stronger. Every chance she had, she returned to the pond and swam. Katicà constantly begged Jana to take her to the beach on the Adriatic Sea at Sablićevo. It was a four-hour journey from Popovača. Jana and Marko indulged Katicà often because they could not help but marvel at how talented she was. Both were excellent parents who always encouraged their children's passion.

Katicà became a local legend with the people of Popovača for her remarkable skills as a swimmer. She was proficient with the backstroke, freestyle, and her favorite, the breaststroke. It was not long before a family friend from Popovača informed Marko that a swimming competition in Zagreb was coming up at the new city pool and that Katicà should enter. Marko convinced Katicà to enter, with Jana's encouragement. Jana made Katicà a swimsuit based on a picture that she saw of a female swimmer from the 1932 Olympics. Katicà tried the swimsuit out in the pond while Jana observed. With a few modifications, the swimsuit was suitable for the competition.

Marko took Katicà to Zagreb for the swim meet and entered her, to the chagrin of the official registering competitors. The official scolded Marko for entering a 13-year-old to compete against grown women. Katicà was four months shy of her 14th birthday. But there were no rules the official could quote to keep Katicà out of the competition and, after a vigorous argument, he was forced to allow her to compete.

Katicà entered the 100-meter freestyle, 100-meter backstroke, and the 200-meter breaststroke. She wanted to swim in the 400-meter freestyle, but Grandfather refused, saying, "It is too much."

Katicà surprised everyone by winning all three races. She out-touched the second-place finisher in the freestyle and backstroke. But she won the breaststroke by four meters. That caught the eye of Mr. Fabris,[1] a member of the Yugoslavian Olympic committee, who was scouting for talented swimmers. The Berlin Olympics, which would start August 1, 1936, was a little over a year away, and Yugoslavia was planning to field a women's swimming team to compete in the 100- and 400-meter freestyle, the 200-meter breaststroke, the 100-meter backstroke, and the 4 x 100-meter freestyle relay. There were strong women swimmers in Yugoslavia for all the events except for the 200-meter breaststroke. Mr. Fabris believed he had just found the right swimmer to fill the void. He rushed to meet with Katicà and Marko. Mr. Fabris congratulated Katicà for her great wins and then invited her to a competition in Belgrade being held the next month. His ulterior motive was to give other members of the committee a chance to see her race. Katicà was excited, but Marko replied, "I will think about it."

After two weeks, Mr. Fabris paid a visit to Popovača to convince Katicà's parents to allow her to race. Katicà was not one to take no for an answer, plus the personal visit by Mr. Fabris was enough for Marko and Jana to give their permission.

It thrilled Katicà to visit the capital. However, my grandfather refused to set foot in the capital city of a regime he believed to be illegitimate. He was still angry about Prince Alexander Karađorđević unilaterally proclaiming the formation of Yugoslavia by combining the Kingdom of Serbia with the Croats and Slovenes on December 1, 1918. Karađorđević then harshly put down a rebellion in Zagreb on December 5, 1918, killing 13 ethnic Croatians.

Jana had to accompany Katicà. She loved to travel and felt comfortable leaving the farm because Yelca and Inga were responsible enough to care for Danica and Pepic. This was Jana's first opportunity to visit Belgrade since she was 14.

When Katicà registered for the swim competition, Jana saw the names of the other swimmers, and said, "You are the only Croatian racing; you need to win."

Katicà did not disappoint her. She established herself as one of the fastest female swimmers in Yugoslavia. After the competition, Mr. Fabris introduced Jana and Katicà to other committee members. They were dazzled with this young phenom and dared to hope that there might be an Olympic medal for the women's swim team in 1936.

Over the next months, Katicà continued to improve her times, and by the spring she received an invitation to be on the Yugoslavian Olympic team. She thought her parents would let her go without hesitation. But that was wishful thinking. Marko vigorously refused. After running away at 14, Marko had developed a keen ability to recognize trouble, and it was coming to Germany like a runaway freight train. He had watched in horror as Adolf Hitler came to power. The nationalism and hatred that Hitler's speeches fomented terrified Marko. He had heard similar rhetoric before the start of World War I. This was the reason that he tried to move his family to America. Marko had barely survived being a prisoner-of-war in Russia during the rise of Vladimir Lenin and communism. Marko had insights into the roots of this new nationalism, which was stirring up madness across Europe. He was especially concerned about Hitler's fiery speeches, which spewed hatred and placed the blame for all the pain that the Depression caused on the Jews, slaves, non-Aryans, and the unfortunate innocents within the Nazi's warped definition of degenerates. He could not understand why Hitler did not frighten every leader in Europe.

Marko was alarmed when the Nazi government went from rhetoric to definitive action by enacting laws that limited the participation of Jews in German public life. Then there was the revulsion of the 1935 Nuremberg Laws, which institutionalized racism against the Jews. It was like a mortal wound to the fabric of civilized society. Marko's apprehensions had a personal aspect. His mother, Jela, and her family had moved to Leipzig in 1932. The Depression had made it difficult for his stepfather to find work in Yugoslavia. Jela had an uncle who owned a successful business in the Jewish community of Leipzig. The uncle hired Marko's stepfather. Uncle Streete kept Marko informed about the abuses that his mother and her family suffered at the hands of the Nazis. Marko had an inkling that another, more terrible war was inevitable. Plus, he worried Katicà was too trusting of people and would endanger herself. Rather than burden his daughter with fears she was too young to understand, Marko gave Katicà another reason why he would not let her go. He had heard that the Germans disguised their male athletes to be females so that they could compete on the women swim team. Katicà was a young woman with classic beauty. Men were drawn to her brilliant green eyes and dark-blonde hair that she wore in long braids. Katicà did not understand the effect that she had on men and that worried Marko. He told her she was too young. Katicà would be a little over 14 years and eight months when the games started.

Never giving up, Katicà continued questioning her father's decision.

Mr. Fabris also wrote letters to Marko, trying to persuade him to allow Katicà to compete. Even some Popovača townsfolk tried to persuade Marko because they wanted to see a local girl in the Olympics. The pressure did not move him.

Katicà, however, had different ideas. She wrote to Mr. Fabris and said that she would attend a team meeting in Belgrade before the 1936 games. Marko suspected Katicà was going to disobey him and, within a few hours of her leaving for Zagreb, he followed. He reached the train in time to pull her off. Katicà was angry; she cried and argued, but her father's decision was final.

On the way back to Popovača, the 35-mile trip was painful and slow for Katicà. Marko understood his daughter's determination; she got that from him. He tried to console his despondent youngster, saying that he planned to let her go to the 1940 Olympics, when she would be 18.

Katicà followed the results of women's events at the 1936 Olympics. She always believed that she could have won. During the next three years, she focused on her education and swimming. Katicà promised herself that she was going to be at the next Olympics and then study at a university. She loved the field of medicine and dreamed of obtaining a degree in pharmacy. Katicà was a very practical person and believed that pharmacy was a perfect steppingstone for her goal of becoming a medical doctor. She hoped to attend one of the best medical schools in Europe, at the University of Heidelberg.

I believe Grandfather inspired her dream because he had told my mom that he had wanted to study agriculture at the University of Heidelberg when he was young. Convincing her father to let her attend would not be easy. The deterioration of fascist Germany and the worsening plight of its Jewish citizens terrified Marko. He continued to fear that a second and more terrible world war was looming. But discouraging Katicà's ambition was impossible. He tried in vain to direct her toward the University of Zagreb. But studying in Germany motivated Katicà, and nothing could dissuade her.

She took the admissions test for the University of Heidelberg in the winter of 1939 and was accepted for admission. Despite Marko's fears about Germany, he did not have the heart to forbid her to go. He still felt guilty for denying her the chance to compete in the 1936 Olympics. The University of Heidelberg was well known for encouraging women applicants, and it had a stellar reputation for being protective of its students. That eased his concerns somewhat. Plus, how could he discourage Katicà? She had been tireless in her academic studies and in her training for the 1940 Summer Olympics in Finland. Marko knew she needed international experience and better coaching. Heidelberg offered both. It was the home of a former women's Olympic swimmer who had been corresponding with Katicà and who was interested in becoming her coach.

Marko gave his approval. Katicà departed for Heidelberg in August 1939 to begin her studies. She had never been happier. Her dreams were coming true. She was going to study medicine at the University of Heidelberg and train for the 1940 Olympics with an excellent coach.

Then, on September 1, 1939, her world came crashing down. Germany invaded Poland. Marko knew that this would spark a second world war. He traveled to Heidelberg and brought Katicà back to Popovača.

On September 3, Britain and France declared war on Germany. Marko believed his farm in Popovača was so far off the beaten path that his family would be safe while the war erupted around them. However, on April 6, 1941, German troops invaded Yugoslavia. On April 10, 1941, the Nezavisna Država Hrvatska, or NDH, declared Croatia an independent state and allied its government with Germany. The Nazis captured Belgrade on April 12, 1941. Yugoslavia then surrendered on April 17. These events led the communist party of Yugoslavia to appoint Marshal Tito as commander and chief of the partisans, who then started a rebellion against German occupation. Like it or not, the war had come to the doorstep of my grandfather's farm and things were changing for the worse day by day.

At the end of October 1941, Nazi soldiers began rounding up young people in Yugoslavia to send to Germany to be slave laborers. Word reached Marko that the soldiers were approaching Popovača and were coming to his farm. Alojz fled the farm and joined the partisans. Marko hoped they would leave the remaining children alone because they were too young. But Yelca, Inga, and Katicà were taken by force. Before they left, Marko warned his daughters not to mention their Jewish family in Leipzig. His major worry was for Katicà, because she was so trusting of people. He took her aside and explained that if she told anyone about their family in Leipzig, the Nazis would kill her and her sisters. That scared Mom so much, she never revealed the secret during the war. She even found it difficult to talk about it after the war ended.

---

1. Mr. Fabris is a name chosen for a composite of several people who recruited Katicà to compete for the Yugoslavian Olympic swim team. When telling me the story, my mom would refer to the recruiters as "they."

DAD'S STORY, PART 1

Jure Antonović was born on his family's winery near the village of Budimir in April 1913. The village is in Dalmatia, about 30 miles east of Split, in what is now Croatia. His family had been winemakers for a long time. No one knew how long, but there were countless generations of ancestors interred in a family crypt at the winery. Jure did not know his exact birthdate, but that was not unusual because it was common practice in Croatia to celebrate a child's birthday on the name day of the saint he or she was named after. The family prayed on that day and gave what they could to the church. Later in life, when Jure needed official documents, he chose April 19, 1913, as his birthdate. He had a brother, Marko, 17 years older, who had departed for the United States before Jure was born. The family had disowned his brother Ante, who was 16 years older, because of some transgression; Ante ran off to join the Austro-Hungarian Army in 1913. Jure had a sister named Matia, 14 years older, who was married when he was very young. His favorite brother, Josip, was 12 years his senior. And his brother Nickola was ten years older.

Jure's father was Anton, and his mother was Maria. Their winery was known for a dry red wine made from a Croatian grape known as zinfandel/primitivo. They sold the wine in the markets of Split. Jure learned the business of wine production from his father. He was taught how to farm in the family garden and care for livestock. The farming and livestock not only fed the family but also provided some additional income.

Jure had a restless spirit; he hated the monotony of life on a winery. He had constant arguments with his father, who wanted him to take over the winery. In addition, the lack of educational opportunities frustrated him, since Yugoslavia did not support the existence of public schools in remote villages. He received his education from a school supported by the local Catholic church, where he learned to read the Bible and acquired some basic arithmetic. He discovered he was gifted in math and craved to learn more. Applying the principles of the limited arithmetic that he studied, he could rapidly add or subtract extensive number sets in his head. He was a human calculator. While growing up, I remember being in awe of my father's mathematical ability. By the time Jure was nine, he completed all the schooling that the church could offer. He always felt that he could have done more with his life if there had been educational opportunities.

In 1926, when Jure was 13, he had had one too many arguments with his father. He was in the field weeding the garden with hoe in hand. There and then he decided he could take no more. He threw the hoe to the ground and left home. He walked to Split to find his brother Josip. His brother took him under his wing and taught him how to be a salesman. Josip traveled around southern Croatia to buy food, pots, pans, fabric, jewelry, and anything else he could carry that his customers wanted. Josip would then go back to Split and sell his goods on the city streets. It was a hard life, but Jure learned several important survival skills from Josip. One was to always be fair. Josip preached, "Never cheat a customer." This was a lesson that stayed with Jure for the rest of his life. Josip always had a loyal customer base because they trusted him. Josip's reputation continued to grow, and new customers sought him out. Jure also learned that astute bargaining was the difference between having a meal that day or not.

For people who lived in Split during this time, getting enough food to eat was a daily struggle. An average person in Croatia survived on a diet of about 1,600 calories per day. The average diet in other European cities was not much better. Farmers had more to eat. For example, my mom never knew hunger while growing up. Her father was an extraordinary farmer. He fed his family well and could provide food for many more families in Popovača and Zagreb.

Dad did not tell me much more about growing up with Josip. I know that when he turned 17, the Great Depression made life as a salesman difficult. He often went hungry. Jure needed to find something different to do to survive. He learned that the Yugoslavian army was recruiting young men, and it was well known that a soldier never went hungry. The promise of plentiful food made his decision to join the Yugoslavian army easy. The army needed recruits for the ski patrol. So, that is where he volunteered to serve. Jure finished his basic training and was stationed at a base in the mountains north of Bled, close to the Austrian border. This was where his unit patrolled. Jure was not a good skier, but he was popular with his fellow soldiers because he was a likable person. In addition, he was a good comrade to go to town with because women swooned over him, and this presented opportunities for his friends. He was charming and handsome. At 5 feet 10 inches, he was above average height, and was the spitting image of the American movie star John Wayne. His eyes were icy blue. When he glared, you could feel a chill. Most of all, he was great fun to be around, which added spice to the dull life of a soldier. Wherever Jure went, his buddies followed. Each leave culminated in new and exciting experiences. His comrades passed the time on base reminiscing about their last adventure and looked forward to the next.

Jure was a seasoned social drinker who could hold his liquor. It was a tolerance that he developed while growing up on a winery. His sergeant Luka loved wine, and Jure was his favorite drinking buddy. They became best friends.

One of Dad's favorite army stories was the time he convinced Luka to wrangle a couple of day passes. They wanted to go to Blejski otok (known as Bled Island) because they had heard that it was always packed with beautiful women seeing the sights. It was in the Julian Alps, across from the city of Bled. The island was famous for Cerkev Marijinega vnebovzetja or the Church of the Assumption of Mary. The only way to get to the island was by a wooden flat-bottom boat called a *pletna*. When Dad and Luka arrived on the island, they happened upon a wedding at the church. The wedding guests had snuck in bottles of wine. They were in a partying mood and they welcomed the two young soldiers. The revelers liberally shared their wine. Both my dad and Luka drank too much and fell asleep in the church. When they woke up, it was dark and quiet. They realized that nobody else was around and that they were already late in catching the train from Bled back to the base. Running out to the docks, they could not find a boat to take them back to Bled and the station. Hung over, they sat in misery on the dock, waiting until they spotted a boat that was night fishing. They called to the people on the boat and got a ride across the lake to Bled in time to catch the early morning train. They reached the base after the soldiers had already eaten breakfast and were drilling. My dad hatched a plan that involved Luka pretending that he had taken my father out for a ten-kilometer march as a punishment before revelry and that they were just returning. My dad was given latrine duty after their return, but the ruse worked. Neither of them got into trouble for being AWOL. This adventure strengthened the bond between my dad and Luka. After Dad's army days were over, his friendship with Luka ended up saving his life.

Another adventure that my dad recalled from his time in the ski patrol occurred on a perfect summer day. He and his comrades had just been paid. They were given 24-hour passes and were eager to blow off steam. The group traveled to Bled, where they indulged themselves. While at a tavern during the evening, a beautiful young woman approached the group and invited them to a carnival just outside of the city. She used her feminine wiles, telling the young soldiers that there were beautiful women, wine, gambling, and music.

Luka was enthralled. He wanted to go. He convinced his friends to follow him, and they departed with the young woman and her friends. The group made their way through dimly lit streets to the city's outskirts. In the dark, they saw the glow of bright campfires in the distance. They wandered through the woods toward the carnival and came upon a clearing where there were campfires, tents, wagons, music, and dancing. Young soldiers and men from the city were clamoring about, seeking adventure and pleasure. Groups of men gathered around each of the campfires, where different activities were taking place: Scantily clad young women dancing; music, fortune telling, performing animals, gambling, carnival shows; barkers, like Sirens beckoning susceptible young men into tents; trinket peddlers and drinks aplenty of sweet wine liberally being poured for a few coins. As they wandered through the camp, young women flocked around my father like fireflies.

My father's luck was uncanny. He never lost money when he gambled. He could immediately figure out the rules of a new game; he could spot cheating and found ways to win. My father loved Blackjack because he could count cards. He was also good at reading people and won at games of skill like Poker. When he moved on to games of chance like dice, he won by luck alone. This night was particularly good. The carnies were getting frustrated about losing money to my father.

Luka noticed that a group of carnies were talking and pointing at my father. He shared his observations with the group. My dad's friends began to worry because it was well known that no one leaves a carnival with carny money. My father wasn't bothered; in his travels, he had dealt with carnies before. He knew that there would be one last attempt at a con, so he asked his friends to be patient. He was confident that he could beat them at their own game.

A carny approached my dad and offered a challenge with so much money at stake that it could not be resisted. The carnies kept a big brown bear in a cage. They used the animal for the main event of the evening, bear wrestling, when the men were drunk enough to part with their money more easily, and when someone had lost enough of their common sense to want to step into the ring. Bear wrestling was a tradition among carnivals dating back to the 1800s. The bears were typically declawed, their front teeth removed, and they were muzzled. But in some fly-by-night operations, the claws were only filed down, and the bear still had its teeth. I did not know what questions to ask my father as a youngster, so I never discovered if the bear had had its claws filed down or if it still had its front teeth. Nevertheless, experienced bears learned a lot of wrestling moves. Generally, no man stood a chance, plus it was extremely dangerous to wrestle a bear. A ring was customarily constructed out of heavy ropes for the event. The bear was put into the ring to begin the festivities. Then the carnival barker would challenge one of the inebriated men in the audience to jump in. If the person were able to put the bear on its back, the prize would be as high as 1,000 dinars.

The carnies desperately wanted my father to get into the ring with the bear. So, they made him an incredible offer. If my dad bet the 750 dinars that he won that evening, then the prize would be doubled to 2,000 dinars. To get a perspective, 750 dinars was almost seven times what Dad earned in a month as a soldier. It was unheard of for anyone to make this kind of wager. His friends begged Dad not to do it, but he did not listen. My father was always overconfident about his abilities, so he accepted the challenge. The carnies believed that they finally had him. No man had ever thrown this bear.

Dad jumped into the ring and faced off with the angry bear. As it circled my father, his friends could barely see him through the dim flickering of the light from the torches and the shadows cast by the exceptionally large bear. Suddenly, the bear charged. My father was very quick, and he used his speed and hands to dodge the bear's body. The bear turned and charged again and through speed and adept use of his hands, Dad was able to move out of the way again. After several more charges and misses, the bear grew angrier. This was the moment that my dad had been waiting for. He knew that an angry bear would stand up on its hind legs and when it did, Dad lunged forward. The carnies had seen men try this before, and the bear would use its great size and weight to put the men down. But my dad did something that was totally unexpected. My father had noticed that the bear was a male. So, he lunged low and grabbed the bear by its testicles with his right hand and squeezed them with all his might. The bear screamed in pain and tried to push my father away, but my father used his great strength to hold on tighter and then used his shoulders and back to gain leverage. He was able to topple the weakened bear on its back. There was a moment of silence, and then the crowd erupted in cheers. The carnies could only glare. There were many side bets on the outcome of this match, and the carnies had offered particularly good odds. Because they were so confident of the match's outcome, they wagered more money than they could cover.

Luka and my dad's friends rushed the carny who was holding the 2,000-dinar prize and forcefully took the cash before anyone could react. The other carnies tried to take the money back, but that angered the crowd. A massive brawl erupted. Despite the carnies being armed with clubs, they were soon overwhelmed by the sheer number of angry patrons. Luka pulled my father out of the cage while the bear was recovering, and they quietly left the camp during the riot. When the fighting ended, the camp was destroyed. No wagon or tent was left untouched. Police from the city finally arrived to quell the fighting, but by then it had run its course and the damage had been done. Many of the patrons involved in the fighting were injured. The carnies had gathered up their wounded plus whatever else they could carry and fled on foot. They were nowhere to be found.

My father had many other adventures while he served out his four years in the ski patrol. After his enlistment was up, Dad decided that he was not cut out to be a soldier even though he had been promoted to corporal and was Luka's right-hand man. Luka tried to persuade his friend to stay but knew there was little hope. They parted on good terms. After being discharged, my dad made his way back to Split to find his brother Josip.

In 1933, events were rapidly unfolding internationally that were destined to drag the world into chaos. Hitler had just been appointed chancellor in Germany. My father, however, did not worry too much about the affairs of Germany. It was far away, and he had more pressing issues on his mind. He had to find a way to survive in bad economic times.

Josip was struggling to feed his family as a salesman because the European economy was still in a shambles from the Great Depression. There were no real opportunities for my father to work in sales. Anton, my grandfather, needed help at the winery, but he was just barely scratching out a living. Fortuitously, my father ran into his old friend Kasimir Botonic at a café in Split. Kasimir was working on a fishing boat. They talked and my dad indicated he was looking for work. Kasimir convinced my father that he could make money as a fisherman. There was still a demand for fresh fish because it was cheaper than other meats. Kasimir talked to his captain and found a job for my father on the fishing boat. Dad was not a particularly good sailor, but he excelled at selling the fish at markets. So, the captain overlooked Dad's deficiencies and took advantage of his sales skills. The boat roamed the Adriatic and Mediterranean seas, looking for good fishing grounds. They took their catch to the closest port to sell. Even though Dad could not speak the native language at most of the places the boat stopped, he was so good at sales that he always found a way to make a bargain. Being a fisherman gave my dad opportunities to visit numerous ports around the Mediterranean Sea. He was popular with his shipmates, who relished the rich adventures with wine, women, song, and gambling.

While at the Port of Vigo, Spain, Kasimir left the boat over a quarrel with the captain. Dad departed with his friend despite the captain pleading with him to stay. Far away from home, with little money in their pockets, Kasimir and Dad desperately looked for work. Both found a job on a large fishing trawler that was leaving for the Grand Banks. It turned out to be a much longer voyage than my dad had bargained for. He spent two years on the trawler, waiting for it to return to Europe. In those two years, the trawler made stops at ports around Canada and the United States such as Halifax, Boston, and Atlantic City. Dad became so homesick that he finally left the trawler in Boston and found a job on a cargo ship departing for Genoa. Kasimir remained with the trawler because he had just been promoted to third mate and saw an opportunity for advancement. My father understood because his friend loved the sea. Dad found his way back to Europe in 1936, when he reached Genoa. He was then hired to sail on a fishing boat that was on its way to the Adriatic Sea, searching for octopus and squid. The boat had planned to stop at Split to sell its catch. By then, Split had become a tourist attraction and the city's restaurants needed fresh seafood. They were willing to pay well.

This voyage was traumatic for my dad because during the trip he and a few of his crewmates had to wrangle a rather large octopus that was escaping from a net. He described the incident as a fight for his life. Dad thought the octopus would drag him into the water, and he could not swim. After a long struggle, they gained control of the octopus. Afterward, Dad swore to himself that he would never again work on a fishing boat. When the boat arrived in Split, he walked away and never looked back. He found his brother Josip, who was incredibly happy to see him after three years. The good news was that by 1936, the European economy had improved. A skilled salesman was now able to make some good money.

Josip set my father up in business. He needed someone who was familiar with the large cities in northern Yugoslavia. His plan was to move goods from Split, such as dates, wine, and olive oil, to sell in Belgrade, Ljubljana, and Zagreb. For the next four years, Dad moved food and other goods from southern Croatia to the large cities of northern Yugoslavia. He had heard a lot about Hitler during his travels and an inkling that a war was imminent.

When Germany annexed Austria on March 12, 1938, my dad knew it was just a matter of time. Then Germany marched into Czechoslovakia on March 15, 1939, and my father knew that he needed to act quickly to keep his business going once the war started. He and Josip talked about what they could do. They did not believe that Yugoslavia would get embroiled in the war, so they developed some strategies based upon this assumption. Dad and Josip traveled to Hungary and Czechoslovakia in June 1939 and developed business contacts. Both recognized that there would be a market in these areas for goods from southern Croatia such as clothing, cooking utensils, and food. My dad began transporting crates of goods to Zagreb by train. He met the black-market merchants from Czechoslovakia at a café near the train station and struck a bargain with them for the goods. The merchants paid in cash and made requests for items they wanted on his next trip. He made weekly trips from Split to Zagreb during the summer of 1939. I sometimes wonder if my dad might have been at the train station in Zagreb when my grandfather and grandmother accompanied my mom as she departed for the University of Heidelberg. Perhaps he even saw her and was struck by her beauty, and maybe she even glanced at him.

On September 1, 1939, Germany invaded Poland. Shortly thereafter, England and France declared war. My dad had to increase the frequency of his trips because the demand had skyrocketed as people started to panic-buy. Josip and Dad hired several more men to transport goods and to serve as bodyguards. Their business grew and soon they had ten men working for them. Business remained lucrative until the Nazi Operation 25 began, the invasion of Yugoslavia on April 6, 1941. Transporting merchandise became impossible after the attack. Germany invaded from the north through Romania and Hungary, and Italy invaded from the west through Ljubljana. The black-market merchants from Czechoslovakia could not cross the borders. Josip and Dad patiently waited until the fighting stopped. Yugoslavia fell on April 17, and the independent state of Croatia was formed. In the summer of 1941, Dad restarted the movement of goods from Split to the north. However, the black marketeers could not meet in Zagreb, so my father had found an alternative route. He chose the town of Esseg, near the border with Hungary. There, he followed a steep trail to meet his contacts at an unguarded crossing. The amount of goods that could be carried on this dangerous journey was substantially less than before the invasion, but the price was higher, making the business even more lucrative and worth the risk.

During a return trip from Esseg to Grod sometime in October 1941, Dad ran into his old army buddy Luka. Luka was now a member of the partisans, which was recently formed to fight the Germans. Luka tried to recruit my dad because the partisans desperately needed experienced soldiers. My dad was not interested. He and his brother had a good business that supported his extended family. Plus, Dad would never break his partnership with Josip. Luka understood because he knew that his friend valued family above anything else.

Near the end of October 1941, Luka sought out my dad again in Grod. This time, he wanted Dad to carry a message to a partisan operative in Split. It was a favor that my father felt he owed to his old friend, so he agreed. He met the operative in Split and passed on the message. Within a week, the operative had been captured and tortured. He gave up the names of other partisans in the area. They were also arrested and tortured into revealing more names. The damage to the partisan organization in southern Yugoslavia was severe. The leadership was desperate to blame someone for the fiasco and decided that it would be my father. Luka tracked down my father in Esseg a few days later and warned him that someone was being sent by the partisans to assassinate him as soon as he returned to Grod. My father was numb and asked for an explanation, which Luka provided. My father had not betrayed the partisans, and Luka knew that he was innocent. Luka explained that he was convinced there was a mole in the partisan leadership. But he did not know who. He begged my father to leave Croatia. Dad had little choice but to disappear. He implored Luka to talk to Josip and explain his sudden departure. Luka personally delivered the message. Josip became distraught, remembering that when my father had left for the army, he did not see him again for four years. This time, Josip had a dark premonition that he would never see his brother again.

My father met his black-market contact at the Hungarian border and delivered the goods. After explaining his predicament, he asked his friend to take him to Czechoslovakia. His friend agreed.

The journey across Hungary was long and treacherous. Hungary was a dangerous place. It was part of the Axis, and the Hungarian soldiers and police were notorious for their cruelty. They did not like foreigners. His friend knew a particular route on which he had bribed police and officials. They avoided large cities and people who might report them. Dad and his friend were able to get to Czechoslovakia safely. Once there, Dad's friend became careless as they made their way to Prague. He had not anticipated the vigor of Reinhard Heydrich, who had been appointed Reich Protector of the Protectorate of Bohemia and Moravia on September 27, 1941.

On a major road, they were stopped by a German patrol and asked to produce their papers. My dad's friend showed them his papers and was allowed to proceed. My father, however, had no papers. They detained him. Dad understood enough German to know that the soldiers believed he was a Gypsy. Dad had heard about Heydrich and knew the danger of being called a Gypsy. The Germans were sending "undesirables" such as Gypsies to concentration camps, where it was rumored they were being killed. With the little German he could speak, my dad insisted that he was not a Gypsy. He told the Germans that he was a Croatian farmer. Dad knew the Germans needed farmers desperately to grow food for the war effort and were rounding them up from occupied countries. The soldiers led my father to the train station. He was not sure if his gamble worked and was afraid that they would put him on a train to a concentration camp. His fate was not clear until the solder stopped at a boxcar and told the officer in charge that my father was a farmer going to Germany. The officer ordered my father into the boxcar. Dad could see that men were already packed in. After he got in, the soldiers kept adding more people until he could not move. He was standing shoulder to shoulder with others, forming a human mass. When the boxcar was so full that no one else could be added, the soldiers closed the door and locked it. The boxcar lurched forward as the train pulled away from the station. Every force created by the train lunging forward, breaking, or rounding a curve could be felt intensely through the pressure of the surrounding human mass squeezing on his body. Dad was growing tired and sore. After a few hours, the foul smell of human feces and urine penetrated the air. He prayed that the train would stop soon so he could relieve the pressure on his sore shoulders and back. He needed to walk. When the train slowed and stopped at the first station since its departure, he felt euphoric, thinking he would finally be let out to stretch his legs. But when the door opened, a man with a fire hose said, "Here's some water, piggies," and then sprayed it into the boxcar. The water stung when it hit his face. He was wedged in and could not turn away. The pain was sharp, but he caught some water on his tongue as it dripped down from his forehead, and it helped satisfy his thirst and soothe his dry and burning throat. Every mile that the train traveled as it barreled toward the German farmlands was torture. It stopped at stations periodically along the way. The people crammed in the boxcars suffered further indignities and pain by being sprayed with another fire hose. Those who were farthest from the boxcar doors got a little water. They were packed the tightest and were the first to die of suffocation or dehydration. The stench of death, urine, and feces got worse with time. My father was close to the back of the car; several people had died near him during the trip. The strain on his shoulders, back, neck, and legs was almost unbearable. There were times when he thought he would die. Finally, after three days, the door opened, and a soldier ordered the people to exit. The fresh air was so sweet that he immediately filled his lungs with a deep breath. They designated this group of slave laborers as farmhands. They were marched to an area outside of the station, where they were ordered to disrobe. After taking off their soiled clothing, they were sprayed with cold water from fire hoses to clean the filth off their bodies. Naked and cold, they were taken to long tables where they were given new clothes and instructed to dress. When they finished, they were herded into lines where soldiers asked their names, their nationality, and their farming experience. He told the soldiers he had worked at a winery as a youth and was experienced in all areas of farming and animal husbandry. This made him a valuable farmhand, so they sent him to a wagon designated for the most experienced farmers.

A local farmer drove the wagon. Once full, it started its journey to the farm country east of the station. The farmer introduced himself as Horst, and in return he asked each laborer their name. Horst told them they were in Bad Oldesloe, and he was taking them to a farming community nearby. Bad Oldesloe is about 30 miles southwest of Lübeck in northern Germany. Lübeck was a major seaport on the Baltic Sea, an industrial center that produced war goods. My dad had no idea where he was other than being in Germany.

MOM'S STORY, PART 2

My mom had also been sent by train from Zagreb to Lübeck to become a slave laborer in a factory, making periscope parts for submarines. Her journey took three days as well, and her description of the trip was very much like my father's. Both had been taken to northern Germany in fall of 1941. I sometimes wonder if the boxcars they were in could have been joined to the same Lübeck-bound locomotive at a major train yard such as Hamburg. My mom said she was close to the boxcar door, so she could get water from the fire hose. No one around her had died, but she knew that there were dead people in the back of the boxcar. She described the smell of death, feces, and urine as pure hell. My mom was a deeply religious person, and she spent long hours during the trip praying for her sisters and those who were suffering.

At the train station, once the filth was washed off her body with the cold water from the fire hoses, Katicà got dressed in the clothing that the Germans provided. Desperate to locate her sisters, she was relieved to find that Inga and Yelca were all right. Katicà could see the twin towers of Saint Mary's Church, a landmark in the center of old Lübeck. They instructed her and her sisters to get into the processing line that was being formed. They asked Mom questions as she passed by a table where officials sat writing in notebooks. Afterward, she and the others were marched through the cobblestone streets of the old city to a labor camp a couple of miles past the city center. The Germans had blocked off a run-down part of the city to create a concentration camp for slave laborers. Another area nearby was closed off to create a forced labor camp for male prisoners of war from Poland, the Baltic states, and Russia. As my mom walked, she saw that the townsfolk stopped their daily routines to quietly watch as the slaves passed.

The German soldiers led the young women to the barracks and counted out 36 women for each building. Yelca, Inga, and my mom stayed together and were put in the third building. It was not a large room. They stacked bunks three high and there were six rows of bunks on each side of the room. The lowest bunk was close to the ground, and the gap between each of the stacked bunks was insufficient. There was a narrow space between each row. Mom and her sisters took the fourth bunk on the right side of the room. Yelca wanted the top; Inga took the middle; and Mom, who hated heights, took the bottom. My mom's friend from Popovača, Ynes, took the lowest bunk in the next row so she could be close by. Ynes was a year older than Mom. They had been best friends since their days in the one-room schoolhouse in Popovača. A beautiful young woman, Ynes had dark-brown hair and blue eyes. Her features were soft and symmetrical. The barracks guards made lewd comments toward Ynes, Yelca, Inga, and my mom because of their natural beauty.

They gave each woman a blanket. A guard spoke to them in German. Most of the women in the barracks did not speak the language, but the guard proceeded with indifference. He laid out the rules and expectations. Ynes did not speak German, so Mom interpreted for her. Another young woman on the top bunk in the fifth row was listening and asked Mom if she could speak Polish. Mom could make out the grammatical structure, which had Slavic roots and similar sounding words to Croatian. She conversed with the woman using basic words and grammar. Mom was able to explain enough of what the officer had said so that the Polish woman understood the rules.

There were young women from all over occupied Europe. Others began approaching Mom to see if she could help them understand the guard's message. Mom was able to interpret for most of the non-German speakers because their native languages either had Slavic or Germanic roots.

The Polish woman was named Sofie. After a week of conversing with Sofie, Mom had picked up enough Polish to have in-depth conversations. Mom and Sofie became good friends. Another woman whom she grew close to was from Holland. Mom became the de facto interpreter.

The guards noticed how rapidly my mom could pick up languages. One guard asked her to interpret for a young woman in another building who spoke Slovakian. My mom was able to help because she could piece together the words and grammar of Slovakian. She quickly gained a reputation for being able to understand difficult languages.

The young women in the camp had to acclimate to life as slave laborers. Germans did not tolerate disobedience and were swift to dole out punishment. Additionally, hunger was a constant. They fed slave laborers a starvation diet. Each young woman was given one boiled potato, 100 grams of bread, and one liter of rotted fish oil for a one-week rations. These rations were used for their breakfast and dinner in the barracks. When they worked at the factory, which was about three miles away from the camp, the women were fed a lunch of thin soup with some bread. The soup was made with a bit of rancid meat, some potatoes, and some spoiled vegetables. There was hardly any substance in each serving. From a nutritional standpoint, the slave laborer's diet derived most of its calories from the rotted fish oil and carbohydrates from the potato and bread; if they were lucky enough to find some meat in the soup, they would get protein. This poor diet provided 1,000 calories per day. The women had to march between the barracks and the factory every day during hot summers and freezing winters. The work at the factory was back breaking. My aunt Inga told me even after 80 years she still vividly remembers the constant hunger like it was yesterday. To get more food, some women stole; others tried to catch the eye of a guard or officer. Yelca and Inga refused to drink the rotted fish oil. Mom watched them wither away. She begged her sisters to drink the foul concoction but to no avail. Mom gave Inga and Yelca the potato and bread from her rations to keep them alive.

To get more food, Ynes had an affair with an SS officer who worked in the camps around Lübeck. Sofie became a cook in the officer's kitchen. Ynes brought my mom leftovers from the SS officer's table, which she promptly gave away to her sisters and barracks mates. Sofie was worried that Mom was not eating enough and snuck food out of the officer's kitchen for her. But Mom gave this bounty away as well. She was losing weight—perhaps down to as low as 84 pounds, she guessed when telling this story. Her friends were worried. One of the camp's officers, Willy, was attracted to Mom. He was alarmed about her health and brought food to her. Knowing that she would give it away, Willy sat with her and made her eat. One of the engineering supervisors at the nearby Volkswagen factory, whose last name was Beck, saw my mom as the daughter he never had. He openly called Mom his little sister Beck in front of everyone. Mr. Beck packed an extra lunch and made my mom eat it while he watched. The parents of the woman from Holland bribed the guards to get care packages to their daughter. She took my mom by the hand and made her eat some food. Mom's friends made sure that she gained weight.

Willy fell in love with Mom. He wanted to get her out of the concentration camp. So Willy talked to the commandant about marrying mom. He came from an influential German family from Posen. Willy was a national hero from the 1936 Olympics, where he won a gold medal for the German boxing team. When the war began, he volunteered for the army and attained the rank of captain while serving on the eastern front. He was wounded and was awarded the Iron Cross for valor. Willy was sent back to Germany and assigned to a post in the labor camp. He was an influential officer. The commandant gave Willy his permission. After hearing this, Willy could not contain his excitement and proposed to my mom one night in late August 1942. She did not say yes, but after some deep thought said that she needed more time to think about it. Mom did not know if she loved Willy. Mom was not physically attracted to him. Willy was ten years older, about five feet three inches tall, a light complexion, short blond hair, blue eyes, a crooked nose from the many breaks he suffered as a boxer, and missing teeth. But Willy was kind, persistent, and would be a good provider. Most of all, Mom had an overwhelming desire to protect her sisters and Willy could help. Saying yes to Willy was a safe choice.

Willy obtained a two-week pass to talk to his mother and father in Pudewitz, a city some distance away in Prussia. His parents were supportive of their son's desire to marry my mom and were relieved that he had found someone because they had almost given up hope of having grandchildren. Willy went to a jeweler whom his father knew in Pudewitz and purchased a ring.

DAD'S STORY, PART 2

The farmers were responsible for the security of slave laborers; they risked harsh punishment if one escaped. This threat caused most farmers to take draconian measures with their workers. But Horst was a good man. He was kind to his farmhands and got along well with my father.

Farming came back quickly to Dad even though it had been 16 years since he ran away from home. Horst was happy with my father's work, but there was something that the German guard had said about Dad that stuck in his mind: "He is a salesman, not a farmer." Horst decided to befriend my father to gain his trust. In conversations with Dad, Horst learned that my father had grown up on a winery and had left when he was 13. Horst also found out that my dad had worked for his brother as a traveling salesman for four years. Dad told Horst that when sales had declined because of the Depression, he had served in the army for four years and worked on fishing boats for three years. What interested Horst the most was that Dad had spent the previous five years developing a business that transported food from Split to northern Yugoslavia and Czechoslovakia. Horst deduced that my father must have worked in the black market.

Horst was initially cautious about Dad because he had heard that the

Gestapo would occasionally plant agents pretending to be farmhands. They knew that some farmers were holding back food and selling it on the black market. By law, the state owned all food production and withholding food was considered treason. The government wanted to make examples of these farmers. After Horst convinced himself that Dad was not an agent, he set up a meeting with a trusted group of local farmers. They invited my father to attend and asked him questions. Based on the queries, Dad guessed what they wanted. The farmers needed someone to sell their food stocks on the black market. A farmer could get ten times more than the government was paying. This profit margin was worth the risk. But, if caught, it would mean the execution of the salesman and prison for the farmer. The farmers had to be careful. But they also needed to find a way into the black market quickly before the food stocks spoiled.

Horst then asked my father if he wanted to be released in order to travel around Germany freely with a sales license. My dad had expected Horst to ask for his help. He responded that he was interested. Horst explained that he trusted my dad and that the farmers whom he had met were impressed. They had a proposition that would make life better for him and for them. Horst discussed what the farmers wanted. He explained that they had developed a network of high-level officials who could grant my father a sales license. This would allow him to sell goods throughout Germany. Horst made it clear that there was some risk selling food on the black market. But he assured my father that there was a plan in place to reduce the risks. The basis of the scheme was to also sell legal goods that the farmers' wives made, such as lace, clothing, and toys, as a ruse to throw off nosy officials. My father realized that this was a good opportunity. He asked about the types of food he would have to sell. Horst described the inventory. It consisted of high-demand food that could be sold easily. The lace, clothing, and toys were also in high demand. My father could see no problem in moving any of these items, so he agreed to sell the goods. He assured Horst that he could sell the food securely. He possessed excellent skills in reading people and could sort out those who could be trusted from potential informants or Gestapo. Horst knew that he found the right man. Dad relied upon the lessons that Josip taught him: be fair and gain trust. In return, the farmers provided Dad with a generous commission.

After bribing officials, the farmers secured the release of my dad from the slave labor force and he obtained a sales license. He began the endeavor by selling legal goods in Hamburg, where he developed a reliable customer base. Often, the customer brought up the subject of food. The ration coupons people received from the government were not enough to feed their families. Once asked if he could obtain food, he answered, "I will try." Dad would bring back a small amount of food to the next meeting and then subtly hint that he might be able to obtain additional food. The customer would always say, "Bring as much as you can." Dad then brought a little more the next time they met. In this way, he developed about 150 trusted clients in Hamburg. Dad promptly sold out the food stocks that the farmers had. Horst immediately saw an opportunity to expand. He recruited other farmers who were also withholding food. Horst began to grow the available food stocks and the business.

By August 1942, there was an abundance of food, and my father needed to identify new customers. He decided to expand into Lübeck.

One day, he was meeting some potential clients and happened to be on the street at 5:30 a.m. as the slave laborers were being marched to the Volkswagen factory. He noticed my mom, who was gleefully taking to the other women around her. Her beauty struck him. She was speaking Croatian. He recognized her accent as being from Zagreb. Dad never thought he would see a Croatian woman in Germany. For the next few mornings, he found himself on the street awaiting the laborers as they were being marched to the factory. He tried to convince himself that he should forget her, but his heart told him differently. It was not long before my mom noticed the handsome man in the street gazing at her. She searched for him as they marched to the factory every morning and then glanced at him.

When their eyes met, they felt as if they had known each other. My dad's presence shook my mom. She tried to persuade herself that she could not focus on such thoughts. There was Willy's marriage proposal to consider; it would be of help to her sisters. There was no time to daydream about a stranger on the street.

Mom was torn; she talked to Yelca about Willy's proposal, her feelings, and the stranger. Mom confided to Yelca that Willy would be able to help her and Inga. Yelca told Mom not to worry; she and Inga would be all right without Willy's help. Yelca was a romantic who believed that every person had a soulmate. She tried to persuade her little sister that she would know him when they found each other. And it wasn't Willy. Mom pondered Yelca's words. Was the stranger on the street the person whom she was meant to be with? There was something about his eyes that spoke to her, even though he had never uttered a word. But the logical part of her mind believed it was foolish to entertain such feelings. Mom marshalled the determination to quit torturing herself over these misguided emotions. Willy was coming back soon, and she needed to give him an answer.

The next morning, something told my dad he needed to speak to my mother on that day. The guards who marched the laborers to the factory were some of his best customers, so he approached the four men as they were walking toward the barracks to gather the slave laborers for their morning trek to the factory. He asked them if he could talk with one of the women whom they guarded. "Why?" one guard asked. My father replied, "I think I know her." Dad promised each of them a bottle of wine. They agreed to do it if Dad gave them each a bottle of the good wine. "Of course," Dad replied.

As my mom walked with the others that morning, she could see my father out of the corner of her eye. She forced herself not to look. *I will never see him again,* she thought. *I need to think about Willy.* The guards stopped the women, and one asked my mom to step out. She did, and the others marched on with the remaining three guards. My mom's guard motioned to my father, and he walked toward her.

Mom's heart began to beat faster. Then Dad spoke to her in Croatian. Reason and rational thought abandoned her. They began the dance of the ages between a young woman and a young man taking their first steps into the vortex of love. Dad was smitten, and Mom knew she had met her soulmate. Neither time nor war could stop the force of nature. Mom told Yelca about Dad that evening. She concluded by saying, "You were right about soulmates. I have to tell Willy no." Yelca nodded in approval.

That evening, Willy went to the barracks and asked one of the guards to bring Mom out. He took her outside of the camp and walked with her along the cobblestone streets in the moonlight. Willy then pulled the ring out of his pocket and held it out. He asked my mom if she would marry him. She hesitated and sobbed, "I am so sorry, Willy. No." He stared in disbelief and asked why. She repeated, "No," and began to cry. Willy pleaded, but Mom said no in every way she could. Finally, she said, "You are my friend, but not my soulmate." Willy took Mom back to the camp's gate and asked a guard to escort her to the barracks. Mom watched as he walked away with his shoulders slumped. He stopped and threw the ring. She could hear the clink of the metal as the ring bounced off the cobblestones. The guard led Mom to her barracks. When she entered, her friends watched sadly as she walked slowly to her bunk and lay down. She began to cry. Mom never saw Willy again. The next morning, Willy visited the commandant's office and requested a transfer to another camp, which was granted.

Soon after Willy left, the commandant visited the factory to meet with the managers and engineers. He asked for their help. The interpreter had left for a higher-priority assignment in the east. A replacement was necessary, and he asked the Volkswagen managers if the company had any employees who spoke Russian and Polish. The company did not have anyone, but an engineer at the meeting mentioned that there was a woman among the Zwangsarbeiter, slave laborers, who did. Mr. Beck cringed because he knew that the engineer was talking about my mother. The commandant was reluctant to use a prisoner, but interpreters who spoke Russian and Polish were rare. He asked for her name. The engineer responded, "Katicà Bek."

"I will consider it," the commandant told the engineer as he left.

The next day, Mr. Beck took Mom aside and solemnly said, "Katicà, the commandant is going to make you the interpreter for the Russian and Polish prisoners." Mom was frightened. It was common knowledge among the laborers what happened to defiant prisoners of war. They were taken to a satellite camp to be starved and worked to death. Mr. Beck told her, "You must agree, or they will punish you."

Mom understood the danger. She also knew that interpreters were used to assess whether a prisoner could be controlled or was too defiant. Mr. Beck begged Mom not to lie to the guards because occasionally they would bring in a Russian speaker to spy on the interpreter. "I know you, Katicà," Mr. Beck said. "You will lie to them because you want to protect everyone. But you must not."

Mom thought about Mr. Beck's warning, but for her it was a simple decision. She could not be responsible for anyone's death.

As Mom was working on a periscope assembly, a guard and engineer approached her and ordered her to come with them. They took Mom to the commandant's compound. She was led into the office complex and told to wait. The soldier knocked on the door and opened it, saying something that she could not hear. He then closed the door and told her to sit, gesturing toward a chair. Mom waited a long time before a man came out and asked, "Are you Katicà Bek?" She nodded and he said, "Follow me."

My mother entered the commandant's office and saw him sitting behind a desk. He was a balding, middle-aged man who wore glasses. He peered at my mom with his cold blue eyes. Then he pointed to a chair in front of the desk. "Sit down."

My mom slowly walked to the chair and sat. "Are you Katicà Bek?" the commandant asked.

"Yes," she answered.

"Do you speak Russian and Polish?"

"Yes," Mom responded.

"Good. You will go with this man," the commandant said, as he pointed to a person behind her chair. "You will interpret for the Russian and Polish prisoners." Mom knew she could not refuse, so she nodded. The commandant then dismissed her with a wave of his hand and Mom was led out.

On the way back to the factory, they instructed Mom. She would accompany a guard and an engineer through the factory and would give the prisoners directions, ask them questions, and interpret their responses.

They took her to the middle of the factory, where guards were punishing a prisoner who was being obstinate. The guard kept ordering him in German to pick up a box. But the prisoner pretended he did not understand. The guard directed my mom: "Tell him in Russian to pick up the box and move it to Station 3."

Mom immediately recognized that she needed to diffuse the situation, so she introduced herself to the prisoner. He calmly greeted her and said, "I am Boris." Mom explained that she was a prisoner and was ordered to interpret. She apologized for her poor Russian. Boris could see the fear in her eyes and told her, "Don't be frightened." The guard became impatient and demanded to know what Boris said. My mom told the guard, "He apologizes because he did not understand the instructions."

Boris, who understood German, said in Russian, "Katicà, you lied for me." He knew that the guards were close to sending him away and that my mom had just saved his life. Boris picked up the box and walked toward the station as instructed. The guard and the engineer seemed pleased with themselves for being able to handle a difficult prisoner.

As time went on, the Russian and Polish prisoners realized that my mom would take great personal risks to protect them from retribution. The prisoners respected her courage. When a prisoner's anger got the best of him or her because of abuse, my mom would lie to the guards about what was said because certain words had terrible consequences. She was determined to save as many prisoners as she could. Remarkably, no matter how angry a prisoner became, he or she would realize that my mom's life was at risk and would calm down when she asked them to.

In January 1943, the Germans moved Yelca to another camp in Lübeck that was attached to an ammunition factory. Soon afterward, she started to have physical problems. She would lose her balance and fall; she was always fatigued, dropped things, her limbs were numb, and she felt weak. Ynes passed messages back and forth between my mom and Yelca. Mom was worried that Yelca was extremely sick and at risk. In desperation, Mom talked to Mr. Beck, hoping that he could help. He told her, "Don't worry. I have a good friend in the ammunition factory who will arrange for Yelca to see a doctor in Hamburg." Mr. Beck kept his promise. His friend made the arrangements, and Yelca traveled to Hamburg for medical care. The doctor thoroughly examined her neurological responses and drew spinal fluid. Yelca was diagnosed as having a Motor Neuron Disease, like the one that afflicted Lou Gehrig, the American baseball player. Once word about Yelca's condition reached Mr. Beck, he persuaded the camp's commandant to send Yelca back to Yugoslavia.

Mom was distressed about Yelca's illness. She believed that she had failed her sister. It also frustrated Mom that there was no way to keep in touch with Yelca once she returned to Popovača.

At this point in my mother's life, Dad became especially important. In January 1943, my father's distant cousin, Father Kordiš, convinced his superiors in the church to send him to Hamburg so that he could minister to the Croatian Catholics in northern Germany. He was born in Medjugorje in Bosnia-Herzegovina in 1914. Kordiš was a tall man with a family resemblance to my father. As a young boy, he had been extremely sick and had miraculously recovered. It was his belief that prayers to the Virgin Mary had cured him. Kordiš had promised himself that he would become a priest. He was ordained in 1936. Like most people who knew Dad, Father Kordiš was a devoted friend and sought assignments in cities near him. This position was at a parish that served a convent and hospital. There were many camps near Hamburg with Croatian slave laborers as well as a community of licensed Croatian merchants. Most important to Father Kordiš was that my dad was living in Hamburg at the time.

Dad's sales license had allowed him to travel. He had a sufficient customer base in Hamburg and Lübeck to sell everything that the farmers withheld. Dad was in Lübeck when he had the guards set up visits with my mom. Mom relied on Dad to contact the Bek farm through his cousin, Father Kordiš, who used the intricate network of the Catholic Church to pass on messages. She now had a reliable way to communicate with her parents and Yelca.

Mom and Dad fell deeply in love. By May 1943, my dad, who was a devout bachelor with a girlfriend in every city, decided to settle down. He asked Mom to marry him. She wanted to say yes but did not think it was possible until after the war ended. She believed that a slave laborer could not get married. But Dad was motivated. He talked to his associates at the farms about his dilemma. The farmers liked and trusted my dad. They wanted to keep him happy, so they contacted their friends in the government. The farmers pulled enough strings to get permission for Dad to marry Mom. But there were concessions. Mom would have to live in Lübeck, and she would have to continue to serve as an interpreter for the factories around Lübeck.

Dad decided to move to Lübeck. He rented five rooms at a hotel near the city center that was owned by a kind German lady named Hilda. Dad used one of the rooms for inventory. He had two adjacent rooms that he used for his apartment. One room was used by his three bodyguards, Stepa, Vincent, and Nikola. Stepa was a burly, barrel-chested man who was six feet tall. He resembled W. C. Fields but he was not one to trifle with. Stepa was a mechanic before the war. Vincent was a skinny man about five foot five inches tall. He had a sharp nose and a thick mustache. Vincent was a barber before the war. Nikola had black hair, pleasant features, and stood five foot ten inches. He was well built and could handle himself. Nikola had been a mechanic before the war. All three had been at Dad's side in 1939 when he worked with his brother. The final room was left empty to use for meetings.

On a dark night, two weeks after moving into the hotel, Dad was returning home. A man stepped out of the shadows and identified himself as Gestapo. He asked Dad for his papers and started questioning him. The agent accused Dad of selling food on the black market. My father denied the allegation. The agent coldly glared at Dad. "Take me to your room," he said. Dad took him into the hotel and showed him the empty meeting room. The agent looked around and questioned Dad more intensely. "Where are your clothes?" he asked.

"They are on my back," Dad responded.

"You only have one set?" the Gestapo agent asked in disbelief.

"Yes, I only have what I am wearing," Dad replied.

"I do not believe you," the agent grunted.

Dad told him he had just moved to Lübeck and that soon he would be able to buy more clothes. The Gestapo agent continued to grill my father. Dad could see that he was beginning to convince the agent. He was given back his papers, and the agent left. Dad watched him through the window as he walked down the street. Dad knew he had to be more careful. One thing that he was sure of was that Hilda and his bodyguards could be trusted. Dad also believed that his customers were so desperate for food that they were not informers.

My father surmised that the Gestapo followed him because of Lübeck's top-secret factories, and he was new to the city. Perhaps he had made a small mistake while under observation.

Dad reexamined his security measures. One precaution that he religiously followed afterward was to watch for a tail when he left the hotel. He became an expert at shaking them off. From that point on, when he returned to the hotel, he went straight to his meeting room, turned on the lights, and walked around so that any prying eyes on the street could observe him. Then, he switched off the lights so that it appeared he was going to sleep. Once the lights were off, Dad snuck upstairs to his apartment, which was on the other side of the building. In anticipation of the room being searched, Dad also added several changes of clothes to make it look lived in. The clothes were rotated during the week so that he could be seen wearing them. Another security measure was to never carry food personally to his customers. Instead, he worked out a complex delivery scheme that involved his bodyguards taking the food to the customer at a safe meeting place in the city. With these added safeguards, he avoided being picked up again. As I was growing up, my father often boasted that he had fooled the smartest people in Germany.

In June 1943, my mom and dad were married by a justice of the peace. They had not recorded the date and never celebrated their anniversary. Mom moved to my dad's apartment and was ecstatic to be free for the first time in two years. She walked around the city; there were no guards around her. My mother could barely contain her joy. Dad gave her money to buy clothes and items for the apartment. Mom bought her first Hummel figurine a few days later. Figurine collecting became her lifelong passion.

In early July 1943, Father Kordiš visited my dad and introduced himself to my mom. He invited Mom to visit the convent where he was pastor. It was something my mom could not resist. She craved being able to travel again. Father Kordiš arranged for my mom to visit on July 23, 1943. She took an early-morning train to Hamburg and made it to the convent by 9 a.m. She spent the day with the nuns in the convent. They talked all evening and before she realized it, it was midnight. Father Kordiš took her to the train station to catch the 1 a.m. train to Lübeck on July 24, 1943. As fate would have it, at 00:57, the British RAF began Operation Gomorrah, which was a campaign of night and day air raids that lasted eight days and seven nights. They bombed the train station in the initial air raid and one landed close to my mom. Shrapnel from the bomb hit her. The most serious wound was just under her nose. Father Kordiš and some nuns saw the attack from the convent. They rushed to the train station to help the injured and to look for my mom. One nun found my mom wounded and bleeding. This nun was a trained nurse and put pressure on the wounds to slow down the loss of blood. She stayed with Mom until an ambulance took her to the hospital where the nuns worked. The doctor treated Mom and removed the shrapnel, cleaned her wounds, repaired the damage to her palate, and stitched the lacerations. Mom was in the hospital for a month. The nuns watched over her. My father, being an anxious husband, was a frequent visitor. Mom's odds of survival were not high. But she beat the odds and went back home to Lübeck late in August.

I wonder what the people in Hamburg thought after Operation Gomorrah killed over 35,000 people and wounded 125,000 more. How long did it take before the realization struck home that they were being lied to by the German government? By this time, the war was not going well for Germany, so the people had to be pacified with misinformation.

The government's propaganda did not fool my mom and dad. They had suffered through slavery, starvation, near death, and the constant threat of bombings. It was a mystery to them that the Germans, whom they had become close to and respected as decent intelligent people, like Hilda, did not recognize what was true and what was government misinformation. Mom and Dad knew that death camps existed but when they tried to talk with their friends, the death camps were dismissed as malicious rumors being spread by the Allies.

My parents realized how lucky they were to have escaped death. If the Nazis had thought that Dad was a Gypsy rather than a farmer, they would have put him in the boxcar going to a death camp. The Germans could have also discovered Mom's Jewish ancestry. Both understood they were still in jeopardy. Dad's business was becoming riskier. If he were caught, Mom would not be spared. If the Nazis discovered that Mom was covering for the prisoners of war, they would punish both her and Dad. Plus, there were the added pressures of food shortages, which were getting worse by the day.

And these were not the worst of their fears. There was always the danger of an air raid. My parents had seen the aftermath of the first raid on Lübeck. It occurred on March 28, 1942, during the start of the Area Bombing Directive by the British RAF, which authorized the targeting of civilian areas. The British designed their payload to create a firestorm in Lübeck by taking advantage of the wooden medieval structures within the central area. Neither Mom nor Dad were near the city center during the air raid, but they saw it happen. This memory had a lasting impression. There were many sleepless nights when they heard the engines of bombers and the air-raid sirens. In 1944, before my sister, Ines, was born, when the sirens sounded, Mom ran to the rivers that surrounded the city center and jumped in. She felt safe in the water and trusted her ability to swim away from danger. After Ines's birth on May 21, Mom had to rush to the air raid shelter with her daughter in her arms. The shelters were no more than damp basements that provided little protection. My dad stayed outside of the air-raid shelter entrance with the other men who waited to see if the bombers would turn toward Lübeck. Most of the time, the bombers passed Lübeck and went south to attack inland targets. On May 3, 1945, however, Lübeck was targeted. The bombing sank three passenger liners moored at the docks. The Germans had been using the passenger liners for the overflow of concentration camp prisoners. British Intelligence neglected to pass on the information about the ships being filled with prisoners to the RAF flight crews. The bombing killed thousands. The tragedy profoundly affected Mom and Dad; they hurried to the docks to help with the rescue. The carnage was almost more than they could bear. Mom knew people who lived on house boats in the two rivers surrounding the old part of the city and was sick with worry for them as well as the prisoners on the cruise liners. Mom was able to use the medical skills that she had learned from the camp nurse to treat the wounded. Both of my parents often talked about the horrifying experience of trying to save the POWs trapped inside the cruise liners *Cap Arcona* and *Thielbek*. Over 7,000 people died that night.

But let's go back in time just a bit. After her marriage, Mom had continued working as an unpaid interpreter for several of the factories and camps around Lübeck. They had transferred Inga to an airplane parts factory. Mom ate lunch at the Volkswagen factory and was provided with the same weekly food rations as a slave laborer. When she became pregnant with Ines in August 1943, Mr. Beck interceded and was able to change Mom's status to a Volkswagen employee. They paid her only a token salary, but the change allowed Mom to take days off when the time came to give birth.

The Russian and Polish prisoners had noticed that Mom was pregnant, so they began sneaking wood out of the factory to carve toys. They wanted to surprise her with a gift after the baby's birth. Despite being pregnant, Mom continued to take risks on behalf of the prisoners.

By May 1944, the people's faith in the German Reichsmark, the currency at the time, had diminished. Food, gold, and jewels had become the major currencies of trade. Dad had to barter with food for a bassinet, baby clothes, baby bottles, and blankets. Mom was given time off work. She stayed at home to care for her newborn. One night when Ines was two weeks old, a dream startled Mom, and she awoke. Ines was asleep in the bassinet in the bedroom. When Mom looked at the bassinet, she saw a white apparition with female features floating above Ines. The figure was circling the bassinet, looking at my sister. Mom awakened my father and pointed to the apparition. He saw it. They were both frightened and were too shocked to react quickly. The shadow looked at them and smiled.

Then it floated upward through the ceiling. A week later, my dad received a letter from his brother Nickola saying that his mother, Maria, had died around the same time they had seen the ghost. They were both convinced that Maria had visited her grandchild before leaving the earth. They often spoke of this experience as I was growing up.

Mom had to return to work when Ines was three weeks old. She arranged for an old widow who lived in the hotel to care for my infant sister. Feeding my sister was my mom's major concern. There was no baby formula available, so my father had to find milk for my sister's mid-morning and mid-afternoon feedings. The local farmers were not producing much milk, but Dad was able to get some through his friends. Mom provided the widow caring for Ines with milk and baby bottles. After a couple of weeks, Mom noticed that Ines kept getting weaker, she was not gaining weight and was listless. Mom was malnourished and worried that her breast milk was the problem. My mother talked to her friend Hilda for advice. Hilda, Mom's friend, suspected that the problem was not Mom's breast milk. She spied on the widow the next day and saw the widow drink the milk that was intended for Ines. Upset by what she saw, Hilda visited a reliable friend on the next block and arranged for her to care for Ines. When Mom returned that evening, Hilda told Mom about the widow. Hilda shared that one of her close friends was ready to care for Ines. Dad accompanied Hilda to her friend's house that evening. Hilda's friend was happy to take Ines and agreed to begin the next morning. Dad bartered for the childcare with food. After a week, Ines gained weight. But the incident drove Mom into a depression; although she had witnessed much inhumane behavior, this felt worse. She couldn't cope with someone sinking so low that they would even steal food from a baby.

The next morning, the Russian and Polish prisoners surprised my mom with the toys they had made for my sister. They had carved and painted some of the most beautiful toys that my mom had ever seen. There were animals, blocks, a doll, and a box. The gifts overwhelmed her and lifted her spirits; this gesture restored her faith that even in

60

the depths of a war under the harshest conditions, some human kindness still thrived. These toys were among her greatest treasures. When she showed the toys to my father, his reaction was unexpected. He wanted to throw them away. Mom got angry. She was not one to cross, and my father backed down. Neither my sister nor I ever knew the reason for my father's strange reaction to the toys. I believe that he was jealous. He never liked men giving gifts to Mom. It probably threatened him. When Ines grew older, Mom gave her a wooden toy as a reward or for a special occasion.

Postwar Germany was a bleak place for children. Cities were filled with bombed-out buildings and rubble. Shortages of food and goods plagued everyday life. Yet, children were resilient and found pleasure in little things. The love given by family was the key to happiness. There was no shortage of love at home for my sister. Ines loved the wooden toys, and they became her greatest treasures.

After the British liberated Lübeck on May 2, 1945, there was no civil authority; the city fell into chaos. It took a couple of days for the British to restore order. The prisoners were no longer under guard but remained in the camps under British care while the war continued in central Germany. On May 8, 1945, Germany unconditionally surrendered to the Allies. Mom visited the camps to make sure that her sisters, friends and the prisoners from the camp were all right. She provided whatever help she could, but it was a struggle for Dad to obtain enough food for Mom and Ines. The farmers no longer needed him to sell food on the black market.

Dad had to find something to support the family. There were shortages of everyday items in Germany, and Dad recognized that there were new business opportunities. He began asking his customers what they needed and learned that men wanted shaving razors and clothes, and women desired garter belts and dresses. Dad used his black-market connections to locate sources for these items. He traveled to various factories in Germany and used his bargaining skills to purchase stock. My father moved the goods back to Lübeck by train and sold them. His friends from the farms also needed goods, so Dad bartered with them for food. Dad found a way to feed his family. The new business became successful and grew. I have always admired my father's ability to keep food on the table and a roof over our heads, no matter how dire the circumstances.

An agreement that was made at the Potsdam and Yalta conferences between the U.S., Britain, and the USSR divided up Germany into four occupation zones. The Soviet Occupation Zone bordered on Lübeck. Lübeck was part of the British Occupation Zone. U.S. and British soldiers had to retreat from some areas of Germany that they controlled to form the Soviet Occupation Zone. But the U.S. and Britain took their time as they sought scientists who developed advanced weapons systems and equipment. By July 1, the U.S., Britain, the USSR, and France began administrating their respective zones. However, during the period from May 8 to July 1, the zones were in complete disarray. Each of the Allies sent trucks and soldiers into zones they did not control to repatriate their citizens from the many prisoner-of-war camps and labor camps scattered throughout Germany. Since Lübeck had numerous camps with USSR prisoners, the Russians sent trucks and troops into Lübeck to retrieve their citizens. As the commander of the Russian transport mission to Lübeck assessed the condition of the prisoners, it outraged him. Occupation forces dealt with the German civilians in different ways. The U.S. and Britain had a no fraternization policy and did not tolerate looting or rape. The Russians had no such limitations. Looting, rape, and revenge were unofficially encouraged by the Russian leaders. Historians have estimated that two million German women were raped by Soviet soldiers. So, the Russian commander sought revenge on the Germans in Lübeck before he loaded the trucks. With all the confusion, he was not at all concerned about being in the British Occupation Zone. He told the Russian prisoners that Lübeck was theirs for 24 hours. The Russian prisoners then scattered throughout Lübeck, where they entered businesses and homes, searching for liquor, valuables, and young women. Aunt Inga witnessed not only Russian soldiers looting in this frenzy, but she also saw British soldiers looting. She was left alone because of her

Slavic accent and because of the rags of a slave laborer that she wore. But Inga witnessed atrocities. One assault stuck in her mind 75 years later. There was an old German man who was wearing a wedding ring that a Russian POW wanted. The intoxicated Russian demanded that the man take off his ring. The man tried to remove the ring, but it was too tight. The drunk prisoner took out his knife and ordered him to put his hand down. His companion stopped him before he could hack the finger off and said, "I have some butter in my sack, let's put it on his finger." The prisoner paused and let his friend try the butter. After a couple of tugs, the ring slid off.

Mom and Dad hunkered down and listened as the pandemonium erupted outside. Mom was afraid because of the rapes. At one point around 3 a.m., Mom and Dad heard a group of men walking on the cobblestone street below. The men broke into a nearby house and Mom could hear people begging while the men looted. When the men came to the hotel, one said loudly enough so that Mom could hear him, "This is where Katicà lives; leave it alone." The prisoners knew where she lived, and the hotel was not to be bothered.

Around 6 a.m., things had calmed down, and the fury had run its course. Mom heard a voice outside her window calling, "Katicà." She looked out the window and saw Boris, along with six other prisoners she knew from the factory. They were carrying bags. "Can we talk with you?" Boris said. Dad and Ines were asleep, so she quietly left the apartment and walked downstairs. She met with Boris and the others. Boris pointed to the bags and said, "These are for you." He opened one up and they stuffed it with gold, jewelry, precious stones, and silver. Mom was shocked. "I cannot take it, Boris," she said.

"Katicà, you must," Boris insisted. "Without your help, many of us would not have survived. We want to show you our gratitude."

"No," Mom whispered. "It is wrong to steal."

"I will not give it back to the Germans," Boris said.

After trying to change Boris's mind, Mom, in exasperation, said, "Take it to your families."

Boris responded, "In Russia, we cannot own such things. Please, Katicà, take it."

Mom stood her ground and firmly said, "No." There was no arguing with her. She told Boris and his companions, "I will miss you and will think of you. But I must live here."

"What a pity," Boris responded. "Then we will take the bags to the bay and dump them in the deepest part where no fucking German will ever find them."

Boris and his comrades sang a sad Russian song, knowing that they would never meet again. Mom said that they had beautiful voices, and she cried as they continued to sing while walking away. They turned and waved goodbye.

After the trucks left Lübeck carrying the former POWs, Mom tried to find Inga, Sofie, and Ynes to see if they were all right after the night of terror. Sofie and Inga were at a resettlement camp and they were fine. Mom could not fine Ynes. A few days later, Ynes found Mom. She had been living in a convent. She was pregnant with the child of an SS officer named Wilhelm. The British had arrested Wilhelm, and he was in prison. Ynes was in fear of reprisals from the locals because of the affair, so she asked the nuns for help and they took her in. The baby was due in August and she was showing. Mom was overjoyed to have finally located her best friend.

Mom often traveled to the resettlement camp to see Inga and Sofie and to the convent to visit Ynes. After Ynes's baby girl was born, Mom gave her some of my sister's old baby cloths. Ynes admitted to my mom that when she visited Wilhelm in prison to tell him about the pregnancy, she found out Wilhelm was married and had children. Ynes was shattered and told Wilhelm that she was going to give the baby to an orphanage. Wilhelm pleaded for her to allow his wife to take the child. Ynes said no. Mom tried to talk Ynes out of giving the baby to the orphanage. Ynes did not listen. She said, "The child would have to overcome the stigma of having a father who had served in the SS. At least in an orphanage, no one would know." Then

Mom insisted that she wanted to adopt the baby. Ynes responded, "I will think about it."

After Mom went home, she spoke to my father to get his agreement to adopt the baby. My father said yes.

But the next day, Ynes refused to allow Mom to adopt the child. My mom argued, "You will always know that the child is safe with us." Still, the answer was no. Ynes gave the baby to the orphanage and left Lübeck.

American counterintelligence arranged for the release of Wilhelm within a year because he possessed knowledge and expertise they needed. He immediately started on a quest to find his daughter. Wilhelm went to the orphanage only to learn that she had been adopted a few weeks after her birth. He then sought out my mom, hoping she knew where his child was. Mom could not help so he left, determined to go on searching. Mom often wondered if Wilhelm ever found his daughter.

Living in postwar Germany was difficult. The economy had shut down, there were no jobs, people were hungry, there were shortages of necessities, and cities had to be rebuilt without resources. I cannot help but marvel at the resilience of my parents, who navigated these perils with a one-year-old daughter.

Mom believed that the end of hostilities would give her a reprieve from the constant worry about a loved one dying in the war. But that was misplaced optimism. Mom had another ordeal to confront with the potential loss of her child. When Ines was two years old, she developed a high fever. She grew weaker by the day. Mom took her to the hospital and the doctor admitted her on the spot. He told Mom to call Dad because Ines would not survive much longer. Mom kept trying to help, but the doctor insisted that she leave the room while they were treating Ines. Dad was on the road and Mom did not know how to reach him. She wandered through the hospital aimlessly until she came upon a chapel. Mom went in and prayed. She heard a voice behind her and felt a soft touch on her shoulder.

"Katicà, don't despair," the voice said. "It will be all right." Mom turned around and saw no one. She left the chapel thinking she had imagined it. Mom then went back to Ines's room and the nurse was excited. "We have been looking all over for you." She paused for a moment to catch her breath and then continued. "It is a miracle. Your daughter has recovered. The doctor has never seen anything like it." No one could explain why Ines recovered so quickly. Mom cried with joy. After a short time, Ines was released, and Mom took her home.

Mom kept in touch with her parents by mail after the war. She worried about the safety of her family in Yugoslavia. The newly installed communist government had taken away all but five acres of her parents' farm, telling them that it was enough land to support a family. The government also wanted Grandfather to sign away any future claims he might have to the oil field on his farm, but he refused, despite the pressure tactics they used on him. After seven years of constant coercion, the government finally gave up trying to get Grandfather to sign the papers. My paternal grandfather also lost his winery and could keep only five acres of land. However, his land was not very productive, so he lived the rest of his life in poverty. My father sent money for many years thereafter, through Father Kordiš, to his family members in Yugoslavia to make sure that they had enough food to survive. My grandfather Anton and, after his death, my uncle Nickola, were able to raise Josip's son with my father's help. Both my paternal and maternal families suffered immeasurably under the communist regime.

Mom and Yelca wrote to each other every month. At the end of the war, Yelca still had hope that she could recover. In December 1945, Mom learned that Yelca had found her soulmate in Popovača. Yelca sent Mom a picture of her and Jako. He wanted Yelca to marry him despite her illness and poor prognosis. But Yelca was worried and, out of love for him, said no. Jako told Yelca that it did not matter to him she was sick; he wanted to take care of her. Jako stayed with her and helped.

By 1946, Yelca kept getting worse and lost hope. She begged Jako to find someone else, but he refused. He kept pressing her to marry him. He wanted to be with her for as long as God would allow. It became more difficult for Yelca to write, so Jako transcribed the letters Yelca sent to Mom. From these letters, Mom learned that her brother Pepic had mistreated Yelca. Pepic had gotten angry at Yelca one day while he was carrying her to the bathroom and accused her: "I don't believe that you are sick; you are pretending." Yelca frequently complained about Pepic. My mom was furious with her brother.

BETTER IMAGE NEEDED

Yelca and Jako in approximately 1945

By 1947, Yelca could not speak anymore, and Jako wrote to my mom to keep her informed about her sister's declining health. In June 1947, Mom had a dream about Yelca that scared her. A day later, word got to her through Father Kordiš that Yelca had died, with Jako by her side. It was devastating. Mom had seen death during the war, but the passing of her beloved sister was the worst pain she had yet felt.

For displaced persons, Germany was a difficult place to survive. My father's entrepreneurship kept the family alive. He found ways to keep his business flourishing. But his sources for razors, garter belts, and clothes were unreliable at times, so he could not always meet the demand. Dad studied the factories where these items were manufactured. A plan emerged in his mind. He wanted to set up his own manufacturing operation. He went about fulfilling this goal by finding reliable people who knew the technical aspects of manufacturing. They guided him in the acquisition of surplused equipment from the defunct factories that once produced war materials. Dad then found an abandoned warehouse near the docks, which he purchased. He and a group of friends repaired the building and installed the equipment he had gathered. An electrician put in the necessary power. Dad hired skilled people, which was easy because of the rampant unemployment. He then began to produce razors, garter belts, and clothing. Dad opened a shop near the factory as an outlet. The operation was successful enough for Dad to recover his investment within a month. My father's business thrived until the U.S. implemented the Marshall Plan on April 3, 1948. As the economic aid flowed into western Europe, the shortages in goods that my father's company depended upon no longer existed.

Dad had accumulated substantial savings, which were deposited in a bank owned by a friend from Dalmatia. My father believed that he could trust a fellow Dalmatian more than he could the Germans who owned other banks. He could have retired on his savings and lived a comfortable life. But that was not an option for him. Dad dreamed of opening a department store, and that required more cash. To generate the resources, Dad needed to spend more time on the road. There was money to be made in rural communities, which were slow to reap benefits of the Marshall Plan. So, he targeted villages in the countryside. He initially relied on trains and buses to reach these customers.

The people on trains and buses were always packed in like sardines because it was too expensive to own an automobile. Dad and his bodyguards could not carry much merchandise on crowded train cars. He refused to ship his goods because he did not trust the people in shipping. My father thought about the problem and decided that it was not insurmountable. Germans were particularly sensitive to bad smells. So, Dad's solution to the problem was for him and his bodyguards to eat beans, cabbage, and garlic the night before a trip. Also, before getting aboard a train or bus, they each ate several cloves of garlic. Once inside, they stood near people and then breathed on them and passed gas. The Germans then quickly left, muttering "*Es riecht nach Scheiße*," meaning "It stinks like shit"; and "*Sie stinken*," meaning "You stink." Dad and his entourage could empty a whole train car or a bus. Having this extra space allowed him and his bodyguards to carry more luggage packed with goods.

Eventually, my father was able to purchase a used 1940 Opel Kadett. His bodyguards, Stepa and Nickola, had been mechanics before the war. Nickola and Stepa both kept the car running while Stepa was Dad's chauffeur. The vehicle improved business because it saved travel time so that they could visit more customers in one day. Also, more goods could be packed into the car. Travel also tempted my father to cheat on Mom. Women still threw themselves at him when he was in his thirties. I know this because, in 1989, when I visited Lübeck with my mom, I was introduced to a woman who said she knew my father. She talked about how looking into Dad's sky-blue eyes would make her swoon. I got the distinct feeling that this woman had had an affair with Dad. Mom confided to me later that Dad indeed had had an affair with this woman and many others when he traveled.

Father Kordiš had always been upset about my parents' civil wedding during the war. Marriage was a sacrament in the Church and had to be performed by a priest. He continually urged my parents to get married in the Church. Dad always promised Father Kordiš that they would when there was time. Yelca's death had a profound effect on my mom. She was deeply religious, and it motivated her to finally get married in the Church. It didn't take much to persuade Dad. My parents asked Father Kordiš to marry them in 1947. Most of my parents' friends were present at the wedding and reception.

For the first time since the war began, there was some stability in Mom's life. Then, out of nowhere, my father broke the news that he wanted to immigrate to the United States. None of it made sense to Mom. After all, Dad had a thriving business. I first learned about his talent for business during the summer of 1959, while on a trip to visit Aunt Inga in Philadelphia. Until then, I had thought of my father as an unskilled laborer. On the way, we stopped in Buffalo, New York, to visit Dad's old bodyguard, Nickola, and his wife, Anka. They did not have any children. Anka ran a boarding house, and Nickola was a mechanic at a nearby Ford factory. Nickola immediately took a shine to me. I was the son of a friend whom he considered to be his brother. He took me out to see the sights around the area. I remember fondly that it was the first time I had tasted fresh-buttered steamed corn, which Nickola bought from a street vendor. He told me stories about him and Dad in Europe. Nickola was proud to be my father's friend and bragged that Dad was the richest Croatian in Germany after the war.

Nickola's recollections were confirmed when I was eight. Dad's chauffeur in Germany, Stepa, and his wife, Sofie, had come for a visit to Pueblo, Colorado, a city in the southeastern part of the state where my parents had settled. My mom had introduced Sofie to Stepa after the war ended and they were married in Lübeck. They immigrated to Chicago. While visiting, Stepa and I spent time talking about Dad. His recollections were the same as Nickola's. He said that Dad was the greatest Croatian in Germany after the war. Two years later, Dad's other bodyguard from Germany, Vincent, and his wife, Anka, came from Omaha, Nebraska, to visit. Vincent confirmed what I was told by Nickola and Stepa.

Dad wanting to immigrate made no sense to me either, as I reflected on his choice. He had great foresight and could navigate business slumps. He knew his customers, he knew Germany, and he was rich. What possibly could have motivated him to leave for America when he had such an exceptional life in Germany? Nickola, Stepa, and Vincent agreed that Dad had been warned by his friend Luka, who was in the security forces of Yugoslavia, that he was being targeted for kidnapping. Dad had left Yugoslavia because the partisans blamed him for something he did not do. Now the communist government, formed by the partisans, was targeting him again. They had already killed Josip in the summer of 1945 while trying to find his brother Ante. My dad was distraught when he got news of Josip's death from his brother Nickola, who still lived at the family winery. Dad's hatred of the communists grew. My dad boldly criticized the regime in public. Vincent believed informers reported Dad's outspokenness. Regardless of the reason, the warning had come from his trusted friend Luka, who had saved his life once before. It was common knowledge among the displaced people living in western Germany that the communist regimes of Soviet satellite states kidnapped people in the West and took them back for show trials and execution. Luka's warning was so grave that my dad believed there was no choice but to uproot his family and leave his comfortable life.

My father and mother visited the Catholic Relief Organization in Lübeck in 1948 and asked for their help in locating dad's brother Marko. Marko had left home at the age of 18, before my dad was born. My father knew only that Marko was somewhere in America.

UNCLE MIKE'S STORY

All my life, I knew my dad's brother Marko as Uncle Mike. Mike was the name he had taken after he arrived in the United States. The reason that Dad did not know his whereabouts in America was that Uncle Mike had never written to his parents, sister, or brothers.

Uncle Mike left Austria-Hungary in the summer of 1913 to escape the turmoil left behind by the Balkan Wars. The first Balkan War had ended May 30, 1913; and the second Balkan War, which started on June 29, ended August 10. Uncle Mike was able to get a visa and passage to Galveston, Texas, on the *Breslau,* a ship departing from Bremen. He left on August 20, 1913, and arrived in America on September 11, 1913. There was a labor shortage in the U.S. mining industry at the time. A recruiter for a gold mine located in Leadville, Colorado, was waiting outside of the customs area to hire workers directly off the boat. He convinced Uncle Mike to take a job in Leadville. They took Uncle Mike to the train station with other recruits and gave them tickets with written instructions. When Mike arrived in Leadville, he was happy that he had found this job. He had been raised in a mountainous region of Croatia and fell in love with the Rockies at first sight. The work was backbreaking, but he was no stranger to hard labor.

Uncle Mike's best friend was his cousin Phillip, who was the eldest son of his mom's brother. Phillip was closer to Uncle Mike than any of his siblings. I always called him Uncle Phillip because he was like a brother to Dad. Phillip was the same age as Mike, and he had also been motivated to escape the upheaval in Europe. Mike had promised that he would send Phillip his visa and passport by mail once he reached the United States. The sharing of immigration documents with friends and family was a common practice in 1913. Visas and identification papers were not very secure or detailed, so someone who resembled the physical features described in the documents could reuse them. Phillip had a strong family resemblance to Mike. So, he was able to immigrate to America using Uncle Mike's papers. Phillip booked passage to the United States in November 1913. He made it to Leadville in early December, and Mike got him a job as a gold miner.

During their days off, Mike and Phillip took trips into the wilderness around Leadville to pan for gold in the creeks. Like many of their fellow miners, they had dreams of making a big find. They panned a few grams of gold dust each week in the surrounding creeks. On one trip, Uncle Mike found a four-and-a-half-ounce gold nugget, which he called his lucky charm. Once word got around that he had made a strike, people trailed him into the wilderness. When he noticed he was being followed, Uncle Mike began to worry about his safety. So, he purchased a Smith and Wesson revolver for protection. Having the gun paid off when Mike used it to deter a would-be thief. He could have cashed in his nugget. The money would have been enough to leave Leadville and settle down elsewhere. But Mike believed the nugget was too valuable as a good luck piece. He always kept it in his pocket during his days in Leadville. Years later, he mounted the nugget on a stickpin and put it in a safe with other precious belongings.

In 1915, large gold dredges were brought into Leadville. The mining company dredged out the creek beds in the area within four years, and the gold panning opportunities dried up. In addition, the demand for metals crashed after World War I and the United States economy went into a recession. There were too many miners in Leadville, and work became scarce. Both Uncle Mike and Uncle Phillip lost their jobs and were forced to leave in 1918. Uncle Phillip found employment at the Colorado Fuel & Iron Company coal mine in Trinidad, Colorado. He met Theresa there, and they were married. They raised a family and remained in Trinidad until Uncle Phillip retired.

Uncle Mike's story was more complicated. He moved to Pueblo, Colorado, where he worked in a garage as an automobile mechanic. Mike excelled at his job and had a creative streak. He loved to modify cars with his friend Cy. In the summer of 1918, he and Cy noticed that one of their most frequent repairs was clutch replacement. People did not know how to drive a manual transmission; they rode the clutch, which wore it out. Both saw an opportunity to design something new. They tinkered with Cy's car and, after a year of trial and error, developed a workable automatic clutch. They took their drawings and Cy's modified car to a lawyer in Pueblo. After taking Cy's car out for a test drive, the lawyer was impressed and enthusiastically recommended that the pair file a patent. Over the next year, as Uncle Mike recounted the story, the lawyer drained Cy and his bank accounts. With no money to continue payments, the lawyer suggested that they form a partnership agreement with him to keep the patenting process alive. He promised as part of the partnership that he would pay the legal fees. When Uncle Mike and Cy consented, they signed a contract in good faith. Neither of them understood the nuances of legal English. Uncle Mike said that after a few months, he and Cy were informed by their attorney that they no longer had a monetary position in the patent. The contract had a clause that stated their portion of the patent was reduced by an agreed amount for every dollar spent by the lawyer. They sought advice from another attorney, who said there was nothing to be done. They had just made a terrible deal. Uncle Mike believed that their ex-partner eventually worked out a deal with a U.S. car manufacturer for the patent rights, but to his knowledge no patent was ever issued with him or Cy as the named inventors.

After the patent disappointment, Uncle Mike was fed up being a mechanic. He quit his job in 1919 and found work as an insurance salesman. Uncle Mike turned out to be a fantastic salesman. He was persuasive and handsome. Looks do make a difference in sales. He was tall, well groomed, had high cheekbones, a powerful jaw, brown eyes, striking features, and black wavy hair. Most of his clients were women who were bowled over by his appearance and charm. As the office's top salesman, his success did not go unnoticed. A slimy coworker named Tony Sraka got close to Mike, looking for a way to profit from my uncle's success. Tony was the type of scammer who your parents always warned you about while growing up. He was a short, pudgy guy who was balding and had a pig-like face. Tony had migrated from Slovenia after World War I. He spoke both English and Serbo-Croatian. Being from the same part of the world made it easier for Tony to cozy up to Mike. Tony wormed his way into my uncle's life. At first, he asked Mike to give him sales advice. Then he got my uncle to make sales calls with him. When Tony made a sale, it was mostly due to Mike's help. He then shared a token amount of the commission. It was all part of a larger scheme to swindle Mike.

Despite Tony hogging his time, Mike was still the top salesman. In August 1919, while peddling life insurance policies in Colorado Springs, Mike knocked on a door and a beautiful young woman named Mary Novak answered. She was 18 years old and had hazel eyes, brown hair, and a smile that melted Mike's heart. Mary was a first-generation daughter of immigrants from Slovenia and was fluent in Serbo-Croatian. He did not make a sale, but he got something more precious. A date. Mike picked her up in his Model T Ford at 6 p.m. that night. He wanted to make a good impression on Mary, so he took her to the Broadmoor, which was not only the best restaurant in Colorado but also the most expensive. It usually took days to get a reservation, but Mike had called in a favor from a client who managed the Broadmoor and set up a reservation. The night could not have been more perfect. Mike met his soulmate. Mike and Mary were inseparable afterward. As their romance blossomed, Mike began introducing her to his friends. When Mary met Tony, she immediately saw through him. Tony recognized that Mary was a threat. Her relationship with Mike was progressing so fast that Tony didn't have time to hatch some sleazy scheme to get Mary's hands off his pigeon. Mike proposed to Mary in March 1920 and she accepted. They planned on a June wedding.

With an imminent wedding, Mike wanted to make a big sale to start off married life. He worked up the nerve to approach the vice president of Colorado Fuel and Iron. It was well known in the industry that the company's insurance contract was about to expire. Everybody thought that Colorado Fuel and Iron was going to renew their existing contract. As luck would have it, the new vice president was Max, Mike's old boss from the gold mine in Leadville. Mike was one of Max's favorite employees. Max was not happy with the existing insurance provider because he believed that Colorado Fuel and Iron was being gouged. Max was excited to see his old friend. The meeting could not have gone better. Max signed a deal with Mike's insurance firm to take over the policy.

Mary was nervous about the meeting, so she waited outside Mike's office. She could see the excitement in Mike's face as he approached her. Tony Sraka, who was watching from his window, also noticed. "How did it go?" she asked.

Mike smiled broadly. "Let's go to the park," he said.

Tony knew something was up, so he left the office and followed them. Mike thought they were alone when they sat down on a park bench. He did not see Tony hiding behind a hedge nearby. Mike told Mary about the enormous sale that he had just made. She screamed with joy. Tony overheard the conversation. He thought about how he could take advantage of Mike. As Mike and Mary were walking back to the office to share the good news with his boss, Tony walked up behind them and said, "I know you made the sale. Congratulations."

"How did you know?" Mike asked.

Tony lied and said, "My wife's friend is a secretary at Colorado Fuel and Iron." He continued, "Before you tell anyone else, think about becoming an independent insurance broker." Tony then said, "Our boss is one and he gets a five percent commission for each sale."

Mike looked at Tony in disbelief. "My commission is only a half of a percent."

Tony added, "The contract with Colorado Fuel and Iron is the leverage that you need to start your own office and I would like to help."

"Let me think about it," Mike replied.

Tony pleaded, "I will do all the paperwork."

Mike and Mary decided not to go back to the office. Instead, they went to the Broadway Café to discuss Tony's idea over a cup of coffee. Mary was adamant that my uncle should not work with Tony because he was a user that she did not trust. Besides, she argued, "You can set up an office without help from Tony."

After Mary drove back to Colorado Springs, Mike returned to his apartment. Tony was waiting outside with a bottle of whiskey. "We should have a drink to celebrate," Tony said.

Mike was still in a festive mood and nodded. They entered the apartment and sat down at the kitchen table. Mike grabbed a couple of glasses. Tony had suspected that Mary might interfere with his plans. He also knew that Mike could not hold his liquor. After a few shots of whiskey, Mike blurted out everything that he and Mary talked about that evening. Tony's fears about Mary were correct. She was trouble. Being the grifter he was, Tony had an uncanny ability to think on his feet. The solution was obvious: he needed to spin a yarn about Mary being unfaithful. The tale began with Tony confiding that some mutual friends warned him that Mary was cheating on Mike with an old high school flame named Dan. To throw some added spice into this story, Tony implied that Mary might be pregnant with Dan's child. He played my uncle like a fiddle. Mike was shattered and angry. The pièce de résistance of the deception was telling Mike to get out of the relationship with Mary. Tony left the apartment feeling good that he had just solved a major problem. Mike was left sitting at the table silently thinking.

Tony's plan unfolded perfectly. Mike went to Colorado Springs at sunrise the next day to confront Mary. Mike started out by accusing Mary of infidelity. Mary could not believe her ears; she was hurt and denied the allegation. My uncle was a jealous man, so he let his emotions dictate his actions. He continued to attack Mary. She was a proud and stubborn woman, so she threw Uncle Mike out. Her last statement was, "I never want to see you again." Thus, their engagement ended.

Over the next few days, Tony inserted himself into the Colorado Fuel and Iron deal because my uncle was too despondent to finalize the details on his own. Tony set up an independent insurance broker's office and convinced Mike to sign a partnership agreement without reading it. By the next month, the Colorado Fuel and Iron policy was in place. It was a $1 million contract that brought the firm a $50,000 commission each year. As part of the agreement, Tony controlled the company's finances. He then spun a story that most of the commission was used to set up the office. But it was not true because the cost was only a few thousand dollars. He gave Uncle Mike a $500 bonus from the commission.

Tony then began to worry about Mike's productivity. Mike was depressed and drinking heavily and it was affecting sales. So, Tony thought that Mike needed another woman in his life. He introduced Mike to Anna, the sister of a close friend. She was a woman whom Tony could control. My uncle began dating Anna in early May 1920. They continued to date for the next month. Then Anna, encouraged by Tony, told Uncle Mike that she was pregnant. It was a lie, but that forced Uncle Mike to propose. On June 20, 1920, a priest performed the marriage ceremony in a private wedding attended by Tony and a few others. It didn't take long for Uncle Mike to recognize Anna's deception. The shine quickly wore off their marriage. Uncle Mike felt trapped and betrayed. Anna, on the other hand, doted on my uncle. The tedium of a loveless relationship drained Mike, and his work suffered even more. After the Great Depression started, Mike's old friend Max was fired. The new vice president thought that Mike's firm was gouging the company. It lost the Colorado Fuel and Iron contract in May 1930. With the large drop-off in business, the partnership was forced to fold. By Uncle Mike's reckoning, Tony had absconded with about $500,000 of the firm's money. My uncle, on the other hand, was flat broke. Mike found odd jobs as a mechanic and a door-to-door salesman pitching products like brushes, knives, encyclopedias, vacuum cleaners, and pots and pans.

It is important to follow Mary Novak's story as well. After the breakup with Mike, Mary was depressed. Her mother wanted to bring her out of her despair. So, she introduced Mary to a friend's son named Stanley. In a whirlwind romance, wedding bells rang for Mary on May 8, 1921. She then had a son on July 2, 1922, who was named Leonard. Her marriage was unhappy. Stanley drank heavily after the child was born and became increasingly abusive. Stanley was an industrial mechanic, but he had problems holding down a job. He took his problems out on Mary, beating her so severely at times that she had to be hospitalized. The hospital always listed the cause of her injuries as falling down the stairs. It never fooled the nurses, but there was not much that could be done about abusive husbands in those days. Mary was miserable. The only joy she had in her life was her son.

In June 1931, Uncle Mike was going from house-to-house in Colorado Springs selling vacuum cleaners. He was walking through a neighborhood near the downtown area, knocking on every door. Uncle Mike had not made a sale all day. He came to a run-down house with grass that looked like it had been uncut for weeks. He thought about going on but knocked on the door, anyway. When Mary answered, Mike could scarcely believe it. They stared at each other in disbelief and remained silent for an uncomfortable amount of time. The voice of a ten-year-old boy could be heard calling from inside the house. "Who is it, Mother?"

Mary stuttered a bit and responded, "An old friend. Come in, Mike," she said. Uncle Mike followed Mary into the living room, where she motioned him to sit in a chair with an end table. "Can I offer you some coffee?"

Mike's eyes were following her every move. "Yes please."

Mary left the room and called from the kitchen, "I have some freshly brewed on the stove. Do you still like it black?"

Mike replied, "I do." As he looked around the room, he noticed the face of a little boy peering at him from a doorway. "Hello," Mike said, smiling at the child. "What is your name?"

The boy shyly looked down at the floor and muttered, "Leonard."

"A strong name," Mike replied. "How old are you?"

The boy answered, "Ten."

Just then, Mary walked in with a tray. She turned to Leonard with a concerned look. "Go to the parlor to practice your new piano lesson. Don't forget that I can hear you," she said loudly, as Leonard disappeared. After Leonard began practicing, she gazed at Mike and said, "I often thought about you and wondered how you were."

Mike responded, "OK, but times have been tough. I am working as a mechanic in Pueblo four days a week and selling vacuum cleaners on the side." He looked at Mary and then blurted out the question on his mind. "You must be married?" He pondered his query for a moment. "You have a fine son."

She replied, "I am married." Mike studied her face and could see some old bruising around her right eye and cheek. They talked for an hour. Mike told her about his wife, Anna. He also mentioned that she had been right about Tony Sraka. He filled her in on what had happened with the Colorado Fuel and Iron contract, the firm that Tony and he started, and his suspicions about how the firm's money disappeared. Mary talked about how she had met Stanley, her wedding, and her life as a homemaker. Leonard stopped playing the piano and yelled, "It has been an hour, Mom. Can I go out and play?"

Mary responded loudly, "Yes, but stay in the backyard." They could hear the boy humming as he opened the door and it closed behind him. Mary looked at the clock. "Oh no!" She got up quickly. "I need to start dinner; Stanley will be home soon." Mike stood up slowly to leave, but he turned toward Mary.

"Would you like to meet me for some coffee and dessert tomorrow? The restaurant downtown is close by and has great pastries."

Mary's mind churned for a moment. "How about meeting in Pueblo at the Broadway Café if it's still there?"

"It is," Mike said, smiling. "What time?"

"How about two?" she replied.

Mike opened the door and left. As he walked down the street, little Leonard was watching.

When Mike made it back to Pueblo that evening, Anna had supper waiting. She asked about his day. He said, "It was good."

Anna replied, "You must have made a few sales because you seem happy."

"I made a sale," was the response. Mike paused. "It was a fine day."

When they went to bed that evening, Mike lay awake, thinking. He did not sleep. Anna could not sleep either.

Mike left early the next morning. He told Anna that he had some leads he needed to follow up. Mike drove to a neighborhood just south of Broadway and knocked on a few doors while people were eating breakfast. He had always found that the best chance for a sale occurred when someone spilled coffee or juice on the carpet. Luck was with him that day. At the third house he called on, the dog had just knocked over a plate of pancakes and blueberries on a brand-new carpet. This was a dream come true for a vacuum salesman.

81

Mike could show off the steamer and stain remover. The couple was so impressed with the demonstration that they placed an order. This was fortunate because when Anna asked questions that evening, he could use the sale to soothe her suspicious nature. At a quarter till two, he made it to the Broadway Café. When he arrived, he saw that Mary was already sitting at "their" table. He smiled knowingly and sat down.

Mike and Mary had much in common. Their marriages were loveless. Each awoke in the morning feeling there was no purpose to life. They plodded through the monotony of the day without passion. Here sat two lonely people trying to rekindle a flame from the past when times were better.

Over the next few years, Mike and Mary continued to meet at different places other than Pueblo or Colorado Springs, where someone might recognize them. Often, they met in Denver. Mike noticed that Mary sometimes had bruises on her wrists, face, and neck. He pressed her for an explanation, but she was hesitant to say anything more than it was a stupid accident. Mike suspected that it was no accident. He did all he could to suppress his instinct to violently confront Stanley.

In the summer of 1936, a friend who was promoted to manager at the wire mill offered Mike a job at Colorado Fuel and Iron. The Works Progress Administration had just been formed and the steel mill was receiving new orders. The mill was having difficulties keeping up with the demand, and the machinery kept breaking down. Uncle Mike's friend knew that there was no better mechanic in Colorado. My uncle gladly took the job. Now he had financial security, with an excellent salary and wonderful benefits. He thought about his and Mary's future.

Mike talked to Mary about getting out of their unhappy marriages. Mary was horrified at first since she and Mike were Roman Catholics. Marriage was a sacrament that the Church could only dissolve through an annulment. Their desire to be with each other became so desperate that they talked with a priest to discuss a petition for annulments of their respective marriages. The priest discussed the Canons, which described the grounds for annulment. There were no grounds that the priest would support. Mike and Mary continued to talk with other members of the clergy, hoping to find a sympathetic ear. Eventually, they took a risk and sought an audience with the Bishop of the Diocese of Pueblo. After a yearlong wait, they finally got a meeting with the Bishop's assistant. He was unsympathetic and counseled them to remain faithful to their vows of marriage. He told them he spoke for the Bishop on this matter. They walked out of the meeting dejected.

Mike met Mary a week later in Denver. He was horrified to see that the whole left side of her face was black and blue. Her eye was swollen shut. Mary had been hiding from her husband for a few days. She hadn't wanted to contact Mike at his home or workplace, so she had hidden out at a seedy hotel in Denver. Mike convinced Mary to stay in Pueblo with one of his friends, and in desperation she agreed. They drove to Pueblo to meet with Mugsy and his wife. The couple owned a bar near the steel mill. Mugsy had an unused apartment on the second floor of his bar. After hearing about the abusive husband and seeing Mary's injuries, Mugsy and his wife wanted to help. Mugsy's wife put her arm gently around Mary's shoulder and said, "Come with me, honey, we will take care of you." They went up the stairs to the apartment. Mugsy looked at Mike and said, "She needs to see a divorce lawyer."

In 1937, the law had changed to allow divorce on grounds other than adultery, such as drunkenness, insanity, and desertion. Mugsy had a lawyer in mind. Mike took a couple of days off and he and Mary visited the lawyer. After hearing Mary's story, the lawyer took her case. There was an abundance of evidence for Stanley's drunkenness. Mike also talked to the attorney about getting a divorce from Anna. He was not encouraging about Mike's case. The only way to proceed was for Anna to petition the court for a divorce based on adultery. Mike helped Mary out financially and her case was filed in court. Mary's divorce came through in November 1937. In the meantime, Mike had left Anna and was living in an apartment near the steel mill. I don't know exactly what convinced Anna to file for divorce, but she petitioned the court. Mike's divorce was finalized March 17, 1939. Mike and Mary did not wait any longer than they needed to. Soon after they received word that Mike's divorce was final, a justice of the peace married them on June 9, 1939.

Anna's brother was angry and filed a complaint with the Bishop of the Diocese of Pueblo about Mike divorcing his sister and then getting remarried. He was a prominent business owner and a large donor. Technically, Mike and Mary were not wed in the eyes of the Church since their ceremony was performed by a justice of the peace. There were no grounds for the Bishop to take any action. But Mike and Mary had created quite a stir in the Bishop's office when they had tried to get their marriages annulled. They had made powerful enemies. The Bishop excommunicated them. This meant that Mike and Mary were banned from partaking in the sacraments of the Catholic Church. The excommunication was painful to them, but the joy of finally being together after so many years apart dulled the pain. They had come a long way since their engagement in 1920.

Mike and Mary settled down and were happy. They bought a house on Adams Street. They socialized with friends and both were active outdoor sports enthusiasts.

IMMIGRATION, PART 1

Catholic Relief Services assisted displaced persons who wished to immigrate. But Mom and Dad needed a sponsor in the United States for their paperwork. Dad asked the organization to help him find his brother Marko in the United States. The case manager had an idea. He knew of a Croatian newspaper that was being published in Chicago with wide distribution in the Croatian communities throughout the United States. The case manager sent a classified ad to the newspaper stating that my dad desperately needed to contact his brother Marko. The notice first went out in December 1949 and ran for six months. Uncle Mike did not subscribe to the newspaper, so he did not see it initially. But in May 1950, Uncle Mike's coworker, who subscribed to the paper, spotted the ad. He brought the paper into work and showed it to Mike. "Is this you?" he asked. Mike said yes.

Uncle Mike knew that his mother had given birth to a boy in 1913, but he did not know what his parents had named him. Mike thought that this classified ad was probably about his youngest brother. He took the paper home and showed it to Mary. She encouraged Mike to reach out. Mike sent a letter the next day to the case manager in Lübeck. Afterward, there were several exchanges of letters between the brothers. Mike was absolutely sure that Jure was his youngest brother. Wanting to help, he agreed to sponsor Dad, Mom, and Ines so they could immigrate to Pueblo.

With the letter of sponsorship, Catholic Relief Services was able file the immigration applications for my parents and sister. As part of the process, they had to go through a physical exam. One disease that the doctors were especially looking for was tuberculosis, which had become rampant among former slave laborers. My father and sister passed their physicals, so their paperwork was submitted for processing. But the doctor saw a spot on my mom's left lung, which he diagnosed as tuberculosis. Her paperwork was not submitted, and she was placed in quarantine. Passports and visas were issued to Dad and Ines on December 9, 1950.

The fear of being kidnapped by the communists overwhelmed my father. He made the difficult choice to leave Mom behind and depart for the United States. He booked passage for Ines and himself on the passenger liner USS *General McRae,* which was departing for New Orleans on January 8, 1951, from Bremerhaven.

The doctors kept Mom in quarantine. Dad visited her before leaving for America. Mom was adamant that she did not want Dad and Ines to immigrate before she could get her visa and passport. But Dad insisted his life depended on leaving immediately. Mom then begged him not to take Ines. However, Dad did not believe that Mom would come to the United States if Ines stayed behind. His fear was due to the constant arguments he had with her about leaving Europe while going through the application process.

After listening to her story, I asked my mother, "If Dad had not brought Ines, would you have come to the United States?"

Mom whispered, "No."

Before Dad left Germany, he had sold his factory and its inventory on credit to his friend Dimitri. Dimitri was a fellow Dalmatian, a local business owner, and someone whom Dad trusted. Dimitri agreed to pay the debt within 90 days. Dad's power of attorney was given to

Mom. She had the right to collect the debt from Dimitri and manage his cash assets, still held in a Lübeck bank, which was over 300,000 Deutschmarks. Understandably, my father did not trust German banks, which is why he put his money in a bank owned by a fellow Dalmatian. Dad instructed Mom to send him a bank draft with his savings and the money that Dimitri would pay back in 90 days. His ambition was to use this money to start a new business in Colorado.

Dad expected Mom to immigrate within a few months. Before leaving Germany, he withdrew 30,000 Deutschmarks from his savings and purchased gold rings, gold jewelry, gold chains, gold watches, three concert-quality accordions, and other assorted valuables, which he believed he could sell for cash in the United States.

As Mom recounted this story, I asked her, "Why did Dad think accordions could be converted into cash?"

Mom replied, "Dad knew what was valuable in Germany but did not have any clue about what would sell in the United States."

Ultimately, Dad could not sell the goods for as much as he had paid. Dad believed that he provided for Mom while she was awaiting clearance for her passport. He thought that by giving her power of attorney, she could make withdrawals from the bank for living expenses. Dad left Germany confident that no stone had been left unturned.

I never learned what transpired while Mom was in quarantine or how she was cured of tuberculosis. I believe that the doctors treated her with a combination of streptomycin and para-aminosalicylic acid, which was a widely available therapy for tuberculosis in 1950. However, Mom told Ines that she thought it was faith and prayer that cured her. Whether it was medical treatment or a miracle, being in quarantine had to be difficult. She was trapped in a facility with the deadly disease and had no family nearby for support. She said that she watched the last hours of patients in quarantine as they struggled to get air, but I have not fully understood the gravity of those recollections until recently. At this writing, there have been many COVID-19 deaths in the United States, and most of these victims slowly suffocated. Each patient was isolated and alone. The magnitude of suffering that nurses and doctors witnessed in COVID-19 wards took a heavy toll on their mental health. The health care professionals tending to these patients experienced post-traumatic stress disorder. I can only imagine the horror that Mom felt being alone in quarantine with so many dying patients around her.

After exiting quarantine, Mom was tuberculosis-free. However, she could not get a visa right away. She had to restart the application process. Mom visited Catholic Relief Services every day, desperate to speed up the process so she could see her daughter again.

Documentation I have found about my father and my sister indicate that they were on a list of displaced persons immigrating to America. Dad's birth date was mistakenly recorded as September 8, 1913, and it registered his occupation as a merchant. The papers showed both Ines and Dad as being in the Bremerhaven resettlement camp. However, my sister said that she and Dad took a train from Lübeck to Bremerhaven. She did not remember being in a resettlement camp. Her recollection was that they went directly to the USS *General McRae* and boarded the liner. Ines remembered weeping all the way from the only home that she had ever known to the large and scary ship.

My father had never been involved with the care of his daughter before he left Lübeck, and he knew little about children. He did not know how to calm a child's fear. Dad got impatient and yelled frequently. He resorted to threatening Ines with his belt when she was not quiet, and that frightened her even more. Her fear of the belt stemmed from an incident when she was three. Ines had been in the closet, standing on a chair, trying to reach something high up that had caught her eye. She slipped and crashed to the ground, making a terrible noise. My father angrily opened the closet door and surveyed the damage, yelling all the while. Ines was a sweet child who was curious. My father's booming voice terrified her. He was never around while she was awake, but that day, he had come home. Ines hadn't known what it was like to have her father at home. She had spent her days with a loving woman whose nice teenage daughter also babysat her while Mom worked. In the evening, Mom would come home and dote on her. Mom would prepare wonderful food and they would play fun games. Ines remembers that when she woke up at night, she would see Dad playing cards with his bodyguards at the kitchen table. The bodyguards would smile and talk to her and Dad would say something nice, but those had been short and pleasant interactions.

My father dragged Ines out of the closet by her arm and she cried. He took the belt off his trousers and then he hit her. The sting of the belt was so intense that she began gasping for breath. Mom heard Ines crying and ran into the room. She immediately jumped into action. She pushed my father away from Ines and stood between them. Dad tried to swing the belt at Ines again, but Mom blocked it with her arm. Dad calmed down and regained control of himself. Mom told him that if he hit Ines once more, she would leave him. Dad knew Mom well enough to see that this was not a threat but a promise.

Thus, being on a strange boat without her mother was terrifying for Ines, and, even worse, she was alone with Dad. Ines's world had completely crumbled. The only thing that she could cling to from her old life was a box of wooden toys that the prisoners in the work camps had made for Mom to give to her. They were beautiful, and they were her only friends, albeit imaginary. Dad hated those toys and now her mother was far away. His anger grew even darker on the trip because he blamed Russia for his brother's death and, in his depression, he could only see the handiwork of Russians. A week into the trip to New Orleans, my father had been drinking. He burst into the cabin and saw Ines talking to her wooden doll. He angrily took the doll away from her, gathered up the other toys, and tossed them into the box. Ines pleaded with Dad to give the toys back. Instead, he walked out of the door and made his way to the deck with my sister in tow, who was now begging him to give them back. Dad went to the rail and threw the box into the ocean. My sister screamed with anguish as she watched her precious toys sink. Onlookers were horrified. My father told my sister loudly that she was too old for toys. He grabbed her by the arm and dragged her back to the cabin. Ines sobbed all night. Nearly 70 years later, that day has never stopped haunting her.

They arrived in New Orleans on January 21, 1951. After going through customs and having their passports stamped, a Catholic Relief Services representative guided them to a train and explained to the conductor that neither spoke English and that they needed help to get to Pueblo, Colorado. It was a hard trip, but the conductor kept an eye on them. When they reached St. Louis, he took them to the track for the train departing to Denver. He explained to the Denver-bound conductor that Dad and Ines required his help. That conductor guided them to the correct track at the Denver station and passed on the instructions to the conductor of the Pueblo-bound train.

As the train approached the Pueblo train station, the conductor radioed the station master to call Uncle Mike so he could meet them. When the train arrived, the conductor went out with them and waited until Uncle Mike came over. "Are you Jure?" he asked in Croatian. Dad answered yes, and they hugged. Mike knelt, looking Ines in the eye, and said, "I am your Uncle Mike." Ines hugged him. They took the luggage to the car with the help of a porter. They could not fit everything into the trunk and back seat. Dad and Ines had to sit in the front with some luggage on their laps. Uncle Mike drove them to his home on Adams Street. When they pulled into the driveway, Aunt Mary bounded out of the house, greeted them warmly, and then hugged Dad and Ines. "Come in! I have your room made up," she said. "You must be hungry. I have some stew on the stove." They carried the luggage into the house. Most of the items went into the basement, while clothes and personal things went into their bedroom. "Where are Ines's toys?" Aunt Mary asked Jure. Ines cried.

Dad looked perplexed and angry. "She is too old for toys," he said.

Mary held her tongue and looked at Ines. "We will go to the store tomorrow and buy you some new toys."

In February 1951, a newspaper reporter contacted my uncle, wanting to do a story about my father and sister. At that time, the arrival of displaced persons immigrating from Germany was a good human-interest piece. He wrote a heartwarming article about Dad and Ines.

As they settled down in their new country, Ines was frightened about being away from her mother. She grew more introverted. Mary was kind to her and tried to be a substitute, but it just wasn't the same. Dad found work in construction and was gone for long hours. The real estate development he worked at was a half-mile away from the house on Adams Street. There was a bus that he could catch with a stop near the job site. When he missed the bus, Dad had to walk. He made little money, but it was enough to pay Mike rent and to buy food, clothing, and other necessities, and to save a little. Ines went to first grade at an elementary school about three blocks away. She spoke German and Croatian, but no English. When she learned English words, her German accent caused Ines to stand out more than just being the new kid at school. The children tormented Ines by calling her a Nazi. When she asked the teachers for help, she received more verbal abuse and taunting. Ines was an outcast. She ate lunch alone and, at recess, the other children refused to play with her. This went on day after miserable day until a girl named Pat befriended her. That act of kindness made life tolerable. The children and teachers were cruel throughout grade school, but Ines finally had the friend she desperately needed to get her through. In fact, they remained best friends until Pat's death in the winter of 2020.

My father's English was poor. His thick Slavic accent made him stand out. Even more so because Senator Joseph McCarthy had recently ignited America's paranoia of communism in a February 1950 speech. McCarthyism was gaining momentum and the flames of hatred towards immigrants of Slavic descent burned out of control. My dad's timing could not have been worse. In 1952, McCarthy became the chair of the Committee on Government Operations in the Senate and of its Permanent Subcommittee on Investigations. He used those committees to start the most egregious witch hunts in the history of the United States. Public opinion was on McCarthy's side until 1954, when Joseph Welch, special counsel for the U.S. Army, uttered his now-famous rebuke of McCarthy: "Have you no sense of decency, sir?"

Dad was verbally harassed and was the constant butt of jokes at work. Neighbors were rude and avoided him. People at the store glared at him. He was a social person and being shunned hurt him deeply.

In June 1951, Uncle Mike helped Dad get a job as a brick liner at the steel mill. He still faced hostility among his coworkers. But at least there were several immigrants from Croatia and Slovenia among the brick liners as well as one American named Frenchie. The other men looked after him. Brick lining was an extremely dangerous job. Soaking pits were an integral part of the rail production process. They lined these pits with fire brick. Molten steel was poured into the pit and then heated. They drew steel out to form ingots, which would go to the rollers to shape into rails. Brick liners were needed to inspect the pits multiple times a day and replace damaged bricks. Sometimes an operator would make a mistake and open the port, which caused the hot metal to flow into the pit that was being relined. This type of accident would cause the deaths of brick liners.

My father came close to being a casualty several times when an operator mistakenly released the molten steel into the pit that my father was relining. His nimbleness and quick mind saved his life as he scrambled out of the pit with surprising speed. He suffered some third-degree burns in these accidents. But he bandaged the burns and went to work the next day.

Frenchie, as well as the Croatian and Slovenian steel workers, loved my father. They formed a strong support group for him. This gave my father the time he needed to earn the respect of his other coworkers. Dad had a strong work ethic and a charismatic personality. He was not shy about his loathing of the communists, who had killed his brother Josip and several other family members. Eventually, Dad won over most of the redneck mill workers who had once despised him for his Slavic accent.

Public opinion is a strange beast. My dad had lived through the rise and fall of the Third Reich and had seen the evil that men could inflict upon the innocent through the manipulation of public opinion. McCarthy could fool many people for a short time, but eventually most people saw him for what he really was.

Life in America was hard on my sister. When Ines was at home, she sat alone quietly. Dad had to work the graveyard shift, from 11 p.m. to 7 a.m., and no buses ran that late. The mill was nearly four miles from Adams Street, so Dad had to buy a bicycle for transportation because Uncle Mike refused to give him a ride. The terrain was hilly, so it took at least 30 minutes each way. Often, management asked Dad to work overtime. When he finally made it home, he was dead tired and dehydrated. He drank a lot of water to rehydrate, cleaned up, and ate a meal. Then he fell asleep. When he woke up, he shaved, ate dinner, and spent a little time with Ines before her bedtime. After that, he read Mom's letters and then left for work again.

Aunt Mary did her best to cheer Ines up, but that did not take away the sting of missing Mom. One day in the fall of 1951, Ines went out to the backyard, which was large and surrounded by a chain-link fence. She saw a young boy playing next door. He waved and beckoned her to come to the fence. Ines was shy, but her loneliness gave way to courage and she walked over. Ines knew only a few words of English, but she learned that his name was Joey. The wonder of children is that they can make do with a few words and have entertaining conversations. After school, Ines would look out the back window for her new friend Joey and would race out to meet him when he was outside. One day, as my father was getting ready for work, he called for Ines. She did not respond, so he searched the house. As he grew more and more desperate to find Ines, he looked out the back window and saw her talking with Joey. Dad got angry that she wasn't in the house and stalked out to the backyard, yelling. He scared Joey, who ran away. Dad pulled his belt off and hit Ines across the face with the buckle. She passed out from the blow. She woke up with an ice pack on her forehead and heard my Uncle Mike and Aunt Mary fighting with my father. Uncle Mike told Dad, "If you ever hit Ines again, I will kill you."

Dad got on his bike and left in a huff. Even though he had a temper and sometimes acted without thinking, I believe now that he was completely lost without Mom and did terrible things that he would not have otherwise done. When Uncle Mike and Aunt Mary saw that Ines was awake, they were relieved and comforted her. It took a few months for Joey to talk with my sister again, but it was never the same.

Mom wrote a letter telling Dad that the bank he had kept his savings in had failed and that his best friend Dimitri would not pay the debt that he owed to my father. Dad accepted that his new life in America would include backbreaking labor at the steel mill. His dream of starting a business was put on hold.

With the sale of the goods that he had brought from Germany, he had some down payment money for a house. He found one close to the steel mill, but he needed to borrow $6,000. The bank would not loan him the money unless my Uncle Mike co-signed the loan. Uncle Mike refused. This was a slight to my father, but he held his temper. Dad began looking at more affordable places in Pueblo County that were far from the steel mill. He was able to purchase two acres of farmland west of Pueblo, about ten miles from the steel mill, from a widow who was selling her land in two-acre tracts. It was the last parcel, so it had an unusual shape. It was directly behind the widow's house on Park Drive. She kept her house, along with a half-acre of land behind it. On the south side of the widow's property, there was a long driveway belonging to my dad's parcel, which was the easement to Park Drive. There was no other access because fences surrounded the rest of my dad's property. This made the land affordable, but my father picked the site carefully because he saw something that everyone else missed. The land was flat, and it had a 50-foot-deep well with an operating pump. He observed that the Arkansas River was a half-mile away to the north and was about 40 feet below the farm elevation. He knew that if the river flowed, the well would not go dry because the water table never dropped below the river level. In a dry climate like Pueblo's, water was more valuable than gold. He asked people if the Arkansas River had ever gone dry and learned that it had not. Dad had been hungry many times in his life. With land and water, he could provide for his family. In addition, the land came with two shares of the Bessemer Irrigating Ditch Company. The ditch had been built in 1892; it diverted water from the Arkansas River just west of Pueblo for irrigation of local farms. A share provided sufficient water to irrigate one acre of crops. Dad realized that the deep well on his farm had enough water for his crops so he could rent the other two shares of the Bessemer Ditch to other farmers. This meant he could get an extra $50 a year in income.

Dad started building a house on his land to prepare for Mom's arrival. He had some money left over after his purchase of the land. He also had the first year's rent from the two shares of Bessemer Ditch and some savings. Using the cash on hand, he built the basement for his future house. His friends from the steel mill helped him dig the basement and a well for the house. Short on money to start the main floor of the house, Dad put a roof over the basement so he and Ines could live in it temporarily. He ran electricity to his home. He put a wood-burning stove in the basement and ran the stovepipe up through a shelter at the top of the stairs, where he constructed a small wooden enclosure for the bathroom. The stovepipe provided heat for the bathroom to keep the water from freezing. Dad also installed a septic tank. There were three rooms with eight-foot ceilings and a shelf area with a clearance of four feet. The well pump was in an elevated position on the shelf and used about a fourth of the area. The rest of the shelf space accommodated storage. The larger of the three rooms was about 220 square feet, the smallest room was about 100 square feet, and the third room was about 150 square feet.

Dad and Ines moved into the basement in May 1952. There they awaited Mom, who had just passed her physical. The ten-mile bicycle ride to the steel mill was even more hilly and six miles farther than the trip had been from Adams Street. The hills were especially difficult to traverse during the winter. When the weather got too bad, sometimes one of Dad's friends would put the bike in the back of their pickup truck and drive my father home. Dad could never count on Uncle Mike.

My father continued to work the night shift through the summer of 1952. Ines had to stay either with Aunt Mary or Ruth, the wife of one of Dad's friends, on days that my father worked. Dad brought her home on the back of his bike when he got off work. He watched Ines on his days off. They were both eager and ready for my mother to get there.

IMMIGRATION, PART 2

After being released from quarantine in March 1951, Mom was forced to survive on her own. By then, Dad's savings had evaporated due to the bank's failure. Mom tried to contact Dimitri for help, but he wouldn't even talk to her. She had little money left, so with Father Kordiš' assistance, she found work as a housekeeper. In May, Catholic Relief Services contacted her about a part-time job as an interpreter, which she agreed to do. With her housekeeping job plus the work as an interpreter, Mom could make a living. She sent toys to Ines, bought a figurine every month, and could save a little money. Finally, in June 1952, Mom took a physical for her visa, which she passed.

Finding passage on a boat was a problem because of summer vacation travel. The first ticket she could book was out of Genoa, Italy, on the ship *Argentina,* leaving for New York on September 9, 1952. Mom was overjoyed. Not about leaving Europe, but about the prospect of seeing Ines. She purchased two trunks—one for her precious figurines and lead crystal collection, the other for her wardrobe. The rest of her possessions were given to the nuns and Father Kordiš to distribute to the needy. Father Kordiš took Mom to the train in Hamburg and helped her with the trunks. He was sad to see her leave. Many tears were shed, and they prayed together for a safe journey.

It was an arduous trip to Genoa. Mom had to change trains in Frankfurt. She was a small woman who had enormous strength, but handling two trunks was beyond her abilities. She found a porter who helped her carry the trunks to the train bound for Genoa. Mom got little sleep during the 24-hour trip, so she arrived in Genoa exhausted. She had booked a hotel near the docks so she could board the boat the next morning. Mom received help from a porter and found a taxi. The taxi driver got her to the hotel and helped her to the check-in desk. Mom had the hotel store her trunks and then went to her room where she fell into bed and slept. The next morning, she woke up early, and took a bath. She went to a café near the hotel for coffee and some breakfast. She then checked out of the hotel. Mom hired a taxi; the driver helped her get to the dock where her ship was anchored. She then made her way to the boarding ramp and checked in. A member of the crew took her trunks and carried them away. Mom was told that they would be placed in her cabin. Mom waited in line to board the vessel and about an hour later made it to her cabin in third class. Third-class passengers had a roommate. Mia, who was from Milan, was already in the cabin when Mom entered. Mom remembered her Italian, even though it had been many years since she had used it, so she was able to converse with Mia comfortably.

After the conversation, Mom noticed that one of her trunks was missing. She discovered that it was the one that contained her figurines and lead glass collection. Mom asked the steward about it, and he said that only one trunk was brought to her cabin. The steward indicated he would see if there was more baggage waiting to be delivered. He came back with bad news. The second trunk was lost. Mom was visibly upset and asked to see the captain. The steward was hesitant, but seeing Mom in tears, he said that he would try. He cautioned that the captain was preparing the ship for departure and would not meet with passengers until the ship had left the harbor. The captain, after being told my mom's name, asked that she be brought to him on the bridge. It turned out that the captain was Kasimir, my dad's friend who had worked with him on the fishing boat and trawler. When Kasimir met Mom, he asked if she was related to Jure. Mom told him he was her husband. Kasimir was excited to have her on board and told her that Jure had been a close friend and that they had spent two years together on fishing boats. He inquired about my dad's health. Mom told him that Dad was fine and was now waiting for her in America. Kasimir wanted to know more about my mom and dad but did not have time to talk. He promised Mom that he would invite her to his table for dinner once the ship was out to sea. Before Mom left the bridge, she told Kasimir about the lost trunk. He said that he would have the crew turn the ship upside down to find it.

After the journey was well underway, Kasimir asked my mom to join him for dinner. He had some awful news. The trunk had been stolen before it could be transferred to the boat. Mom was heartbroken and told Kasimir that it contained her most precious possessions. He consoled her and said he would radio back to the port to see if the harbor master could do anything. During the meal, they talked extensively about what happened to Dad during the war. Kasimir heard about my mom's history as an interpreter and learned about the training she had in nursing.

As the journey began, the captain was warned about severe storms in the Atlantic. He knew that this would be a difficult crossing. For the first four days, the seas were calm, but he dreaded the foul weather ahead. On the fifth day, dark clouds appeared and the wind grew worse. The passengers began to visit the infirmary in droves with sea sickness. My mom loved the ocean and did not mind the rocking motion of the boat. The ocean waves fascinated her and the rolling movement relaxed her. Mia was seasick and could not hold down food. Mom nursed her. In the meantime, the captain was facing a crisis. About a third of the passengers had already visited the infirmary, and the staff was overwhelmed. Kasimir decided that he needed to find people with nursing experience among the passengers to help care for the sick. The first person he thought of was my mom and, like always, she was ready to help.

Mom worked 12-hour shifts in the infirmary caring for sick passengers. Kasimir sent her a basket of fresh fruit every evening in appreciation for her help. After her first day in the clinic, Mom came back to the room to find an empty fruit basket and a card from the captain addressed to Katicà, with a note thanking her. Mia had recovered and had eaten all the fruit. Mom told Mia that the fruit basket belonged to her. Mia apologized but claimed that she was starving after not eating for so long. Mom felt pity and gave Mia permission to take a few pieces of fruit the next time the captain sent a basket. The following night, when Mom returned from the clinic, there was an empty basket and a thank-you card from the captain. Mom scolded Mia for not leaving any fruit. Mia explained that she couldn't stop herself. Mom saw that Mia had no intention of saving any fruit. But Mom was too exhausted and decided that it wasn't worth it to escalate the confrontation. For the remainder of the voyage, after she came back to her cabin from the clinic, she found a basket devoid of fruit.

The storm subsided on the night of September 17. The next day, the ship arrived in New York. As Mom departed from the boat, Kasimir stopped and thanked her. He handed her a letter to take to my father. Mom went through customs. Inga and Mom's uncle, Valentine, Jana's brother, were waiting for her. They spent a few hours with Mom and then brought her to Grand Central Terminal. There she caught the train bound for Denver, Colorado. Mom was impressed with the green trees as the train made its way to Kansas City. Parts of the journey reminded her of the farm where she grew up and other parts of the Rhine River valley. As the train passed through Kansas and eastern Colorado, the terrain went from the beautiful green color that she loved to the brown and dingy colors of the high plains in late summer. She became sad. *How can anyone live in a place like this?* she thought. Mom changed trains in Denver for the last leg of her journey to Pueblo. The Pueblo train station was near the Arkansas

River, and at least the sight of water perked up her spirits. When the train stopped, she looked out the window and saw Dad and Ines waving. Her heart leaped at the sight of her daughter. Seeing Ines wiped away any doubts that she might have had.

A SON

Dad had made progress on the main level of the house before Mom arrived, but it was far from complete. Only two of the walls were up when he brought her home. My mother was disappointed in the condition of her future house. Living in a basement was a difficult transition, but she maintained a positive attitude. It was a small, crowded space. Mom had to cut wood every day for the stove in order to cook and to provide heat, because it was getting colder. By Christmas, Dad had completed all four walls, put in the exterior doors and windows, constructed the rafters, and put the roof on. But the interior of the house required a lot of work. The rooms on the main floor lacked framing and drywall. The kitchen needed plumbing, and the house required a natural-gas heating system with ductwork. Dad had run out of money. Plus, Mom was pregnant with me.

Ines was young at the time and doesn't recall much about Mom's transition into her new life in Colorado. All that Ines remembers is being happy again. With Mom watching over her, Ines began to develop a better relationship with Dad. When I asked Mom questions about this period in her life, she did not want to talk about it. Knowing that Mom was a glass-half-full person, I believe she endeavored to make the best of her new life and did not wish to look backward. The other burden was that Mom loved to be around people and craved conversation. But none of the neighbors wanted to talk to her. They were hostile because she was Slavic and Roman Catholic. Aunt Mary was her only friend. She desperately tried to find friends elsewhere. Eventually, the wives of my dad's buddies from the mill socialized with Mom. She began attending Mass at the local Catholic church about two miles away from the farm. Soon, she made more acquaintances among the parishioners. Mom also grew close to the community of nuns at the church's convent. Her social circle grew little by little, but it was smaller than what she was used to. But at least she did not feel alone anymore.

My dad scrimped and saved to complete the house. He tried to get a loan, but all the banks he went to denied him because he had no co-signer. Uncle Mike always refused to co-sign. My family still lived in the basement on July 2, 1953. On that day, Aunt Mary had convinced Mom to see *Young Bess* with her at the movie theater. Mom had been stuck in the basement for a long while. After eight and a half months of pregnancy, she felt trapped and was happy to get out. In the middle of the movie, at around 1 p.m., her water broke. Mary rushed Mom to the hospital. Mary called the friend who was watching Ines for the afternoon and told her that Mom had just gone into labor. Mary arranged for her to watch Ines overnight. There was no phone on the farm, so Mary called Uncle Mike to find my father. Mary stayed at the hospital with Mom. Dad had been working overtime that day, so Uncle Mike did not find him at home. He continued to search for Dad at other likely places. When my father got home at 2 p.m., he saw a note from Mom indicating that she was out with Mary and would return later in the afternoon. Dad then fell asleep. At 5 p.m., Uncle Mike came back to our house to see if Dad was home. He found my father in bed. Uncle Mike woke him up and told him that Mom was at the hospital in labor.

Mike drove Dad to the hospital. They met Mary in the waiting room. All three of them paced the floor until I was born at 9:31 p.m. About a half-hour later, a nurse entered the waiting room and asked the group to follow her. She took them to the maternity-ward viewing area and pointed to the bassinet I was in. My dad said that when he looked at me for the first time, I yawned.

Some babies have rich parents, some are the children of royalty, some have middle-class parents, and some are the children of the poor. As adults, people often wish that they had wealthy parents or were the offspring of royalty. I was the child of a poor immigrant family. Still, I don't think I could have been luckier.

With a new baby to care for, money was tight for my parents. Mom had to take a job at the hospital. She had hoped that the hospital would allow her to work with patients, but they only permitted her to wash pots and pans. Uncle Mike and Aunt Mary traded their house on Adams Street for a house in a new real estate development on Westwood Lane. The house was about a quarter-mile from our farm. So, Mom walked to Westwood Lane with Ines and me, dropped us off on her way to work, and picked us up on her way back. Dad continued the construction on the main floor of our house little by little. When I was five months old, the bank finally loaned Dad $2,500 to complete the house. Afterward, the remaining construction proceeded quickly. We moved out of the basement in February 1954, which was fortunate, because I started walking when I was eight months old. I was also an early talker. My parents had their hands full because I was rambunctious.

Dad was right about the well; the farm had bumper crops every year because there was plenty of water. The family grew vegetables, canned the produce, made sauerkraut, and sold the excess. The income from the sale of vegetables was used to buy lumber to build a chicken coop and a barn. Dad also purchased livestock such as chickens, goats, rabbits, and pigs. Mom and Dad went to the grocery store only to buy items that the farm couldn't produce such as flour, coffee, salt, pepper, milk, and sugar. The chaos in my parents' lives had settled down.

Mom's job at the hospital mentally wore on her. The work was not rewarding, and Ines told me she came home sad and drained. When I was a year and a half old, Mom found a job as a maid and cook for a wonderful family. The husband's name was Aub and the wife's name was Harriet. They had two boys named Arlen (the oldest by two years) and Larry. The job paid 55 cents an hour, and Mom worked 12-hour days, but she loved the family and felt satisfied at the end of the day. But it was still an ordeal. She caught a bus at 5:30 a.m. and traveled the five miles from our home in Pueblo County to the home of her client so she could arrive in time to prepare breakfast, pack lunches for the children, and get the two boys ready for school. She spent the day cleaning the large house, doing laundry, and getting dinner ready after everyone left. When Arlen and Larry returned from school, Mom would greet them and would prepare their after-school snacks. She would serve dinner at 5:15 p.m. and then wash dishes. Afterward, it was an all-out rush to catch the 6:15 p.m. bus. Mom would arrive home at around 6:45 p.m.; I would wait for her at the door. When she opened the door and saw me, she would light up no matter how worn and tired she felt.

After years of riding a bike, Dad purchased a used 1949 black Chevrolet deluxe sedan in January 1956. The car was his pride and joy. He could now drive to work. Things were going well until the fall of 1956. One day, after Dad left for his night shift at 6 p.m., Mom picked up the mail on her way home from work. There was a letter from Germany addressed to my father. Mom grew curious because it had a fragrance like lilacs. She resisted opening the letter, but she could not stop thinking about it. Her curiosity finally did get the best of her, so she opened it. Inside was a picture of an attractive woman along with a letter. The letter was from someone named Helga. It said my father had promised to send for her once he was in America. Helga had spent years tracking Dad down. She was waiting for him to bring her to America like he had promised.

Mom was furious and wanted to confront Dad as soon as he came home. After her temper quelled, she hatched another scheme. She put Helga's picture in a frame and set it on the nightstand next to Dad's side of the bed. When Dad came home and fell asleep, Mom laid awake waiting for the morning to come so that Dad would see the picture. Morning came and went, but my father had no reaction. That evening, he came home from work and fell asleep. The next morning there was still no reaction. Mom's patience wore thin. She could not contain herself, so she confronted Dad with the picture and the letter. Dad denied knowing the woman and did not budge from his story. Mom was angry for a few weeks. But she forgave Dad.

The next year had an ominous beginning. In the spring of 1957, Mom woke up to the sound of an owl hooting outside her bedroom window. Owls had never come around the house before or since. Mom was shaken and could not get back to sleep. Even though I was almost four, I still remember waking up and hearing Mom talking to Dad, who was trying to calm her down. I heard the owl as well. When Mom was a little girl, she remembered an old wives' tale that when an owl hoots outside the house, someone close to you will die. The story gave me nightmares. We had just put in a telephone, and a few hours later, I remember hearing it ring at 3 a.m. It was Aunt Inga, who reported that my grandfather Marko had died. He was 75 and was ill because he had refused medical treatment for hyperplasia of the prostate. This occurs when the prostate increases in size and blocks the urethra. This condition leads to kidney failure and death. When I met my Uncle Pepic years later, he told me that Grandfather was in great pain during his last days and that Grandmother begged him to let the doctor treat him. The night before he died, Grandfather knew that he did not have long to live. He asked Pepic to drink some slivovitz with him. Grandfather made Pepic promise to take care of his mother. After hearing the news of her father's death, Mom was inconsolable. She had been her father's favorite, and he was hers. It was a difficult time for all of us.

A few months later, there was a bird outside Mom's bedroom window pecking on the windowsill during the night. Mom woke up in a panic. There were superstitions she remembered from her childhood about birds trying to get into the house at night. She was told that they were the spirits of souls who had passed away seeking their loved ones. The next day Aunt Inga called to tell Mom that my grandma Jana had died the night before. Inga said that Jana missed Marko so much that she lost her will to live. She was 64.

I remember that soon after my grandmother died, Aunt Mary told my parents that she was concerned because I did not speak English. At home, Mom, Dad and Ines spoke only Croatian. English was not Mary's first language, and she believed that fact had held her back in school. She still carried old wounds from childhood, when kids had made fun of her accent. Mary told Mom that she did not want that happening to me. Mary had me watch children's television programs at her house to improve my English. She did not allow me to speak any Croatian around her. She also convinced my mom that I should speak only English at home. Mom believed it was important as well. When Mom insisted that the family speak only English to me, Dad argued with her. But Mom was too stubborn to lose. From that point on, if I spoke Croatian, Mom reminded me to speak English. When Mom and Ines talked to me, it was in English. Dad was too obstinate, so he spoke only Croatian to me. But I was allowed to respond only in English.

My intensive English training did have one side benefit. It helped my parents get ready for their citizenship test in the fall of 1957. I recall that Mom and Dad were preparing for a party in anticipation of their naturalization. Mom was an excellent pastry chef, and her strudels, *potica,* cakes, cookies, and tortes were spectacular. Her cheese strudel, apple strudel, and *potica* were particularly prized by family friends. As a four-year-old, I wanted to learn how to make pastry, so I pestered Mom one day while she was baking for the celebration. Mom showed me how to make *potica.* She used the kitchen table to roll her dough until it was paper thin. Mom then gave me enough unworked dough to make a half-loaf of *potica* and allowed me to roll the dough on the kitchen floor beside her until I made it paper thin. We each covered the finished dough with melted butter followed by layers of ground nuts, raisins, honey, and lemon juice. She then started at one edge and began rolling the dough until it formed a large, cylindrical loaf. I copied her and made a half-sized loaf. I was proud of the *potica* I had just made. Mom placed it on the kitchen counter next to her unbaked loaf. Mom then made nine more loves, after which she preheated the oven. I watched her put five of the loaves in the oven and bake them. Mine was not one. When the first five loaves were golden brown, she pulled them out and laid them on the counter to cool. She then placed her remaining five loaves in the oven. I was upset that she did not put mine in to bake as well. So, to placate me, Mom placed my half-loaf in the oven. When these loaves were golden brown, she put them on the counter to cool. My *potica* looked so good, I could hardly wait to taste it. I left the kitchen to play and patiently waited. In the meantime, Dad was getting ready to go to the mill for his shift. He saw the *potica* on the counter and spotted the half-loaf. He decided that it was the perfect size to give to his boss. When I went back in the kitchen to check on my half-loaf of *potica,* it was gone. I was furious. I thought that Mom had thrown it away. But Mom did not know what had happened to it and tried to calm me down. I fell asleep, but I was still angry. We found out the next morning about my dad's gift to his boss. Mom was horrified because I had made the *potica* on the kitchen floor and who knew how much dirt and hair got into it. I was ecstatic that Dad gave it to his boss. Dad felt like a fool.

Mom and Dad went to the courthouse the next day to take their citizenship test and oath. They both passed and were sworn in as citizens of the United States. This was their proudest moment. They had a huge party with friends and family. Dad could not stop smiling. Both of them loved America and always celebrated Independence Day with reverence. This was the first time that my parents would be able to experience the pleasure of voting for their leaders. They believed that voting was the sacred duty of every citizen and would never miss an election. Ines had to wait until she turned 17 to take the citizenship test.

In the spring of 1958, Dad finished building a two-car garage and a small two-bedroom, one-bath house on the property that he rented for supplemental income. The garage gave him the space that he needed for his next big plan. He constantly complained about the cost of wine. Dad then learned it was legal to make 200 gallons of wine a year. The extra space in the garage allowed him to set up his own small winery, where he used the skills he had acquired as a child at his father's knee. Dad purchased oak barrels and a grape crusher. He stored his barrels and wine-making equipment on one side of the garage. In September, he bought grapes in bulk from the brother of Uncle Mike's ex-wife, Ann, who owned a fruit distribution company. Dad chose two California grapes, zinfandel for his red wine and muscatel for his white wine. They reminded him of the grapes that his father had grown in his vineyard. Dad cleared out the large room in the basement and carried 12 open-top oak barrels, used for crushing and fermenting the grapes, down the narrow stairway into the basement. The top head on these barrels were open. Another characteristic of the fermenting barrel was that near the bottom of its side, there was a hole sealed by a wooden plug and wax that was used to remove the fermented juice. Dad used the well-pump room as a permanent site for the storage barrels that contained the finished product. The fruit company delivered a huge shipment and Dad had a group of his friends carry the crates into the basement. He opened the crates and put the grapes in the crusher, which was placed on the top of the fermenting barrel. Then he used the hand crank to crush the grapes and the juice and rind flowed into the barrel. When he finished the crushing process, there were six barrels with zinfandel juice and six barrels with muscatel juice. The natural yeast on the grape's skin initiated the fermentation process. Dad put cheesecloth over the barrels and let the juice ferment for two weeks. I remember the smell of fermenting wine permeating throughout the house. My clothes smelled like wine and the kids at school made comments about it.

Dad tested the alcohol content by taste to determine when the wine was ready. After the grapes had completed the fermentation, he put spigots in the holes at the bottom of the fermenting barrels to transfer the wine into steel pots that were large enough to hold five gallons. He carried vessels across the hall and poured the wine into a storage barrel. The storage barrels were different from the fermentation barrels. They were set on their side on top of a stand.

There was a round hole, called a bung hole, in the side of the storage barrel. The barrel was rotated until the bung hole was on top. The bung hole was used to fill the barrel with new wine. Once the barrels were filled, Dad sealed the bung hole with a wooden plug and wax. On the front head of the storage barrel, there was a hole used for a spigot. While aging the wine, the spigot hole was sealed with a solid wooden plug and wax. When Dad was ready to tap the barrel, he put a large metal basin underneath the spigot hole and then skillfully knocked out the plug with a wooden hammer. He quickly stopped the flow of wine by inserting a wooden spigot.

Dad also had a process for making "seconds," better known as a second run, using the rind that remained in the fermentation barrels. He added water and sugar to the rind, and then allowed that mixture to ferment. Dad tasted the juice once or twice a day and when it was ready, he poured the wine into designated storage barrels for the "seconds". My father finished the process by using a press to squeeze the remaining liquid out of the rind, which he then added to the "seconds" barrels.

You could drink muscatel right away, so Dad tapped one barrel containing the first squeeze. He also tapped a barrel of the zinfandel seconds because this wine did not improve with age. It was your basic rot gut. However, the first squeeze of zinfandel needed to be aged a minimum of three months before it was drinkable. Dad saved the muscatel seconds until all the other barrels were empty. This wine actually tasted better than the first squeeze. Mom and Dad additionally kept five-gallon glass jars filled with previous vintages sealed with a cork and wax for additional aging. These containers were very precious and were opened only on special occasions.

As time went on, I became proficient in English, but the lack of an accent did not change our neighbors' attitude. The families who lived around us still did not let their children play with me. They shunned my whole family. I recall meeting Greg after my fifth birthday. He was a year older and one of my nearest neighbors. His father and several of his close family members had purchased two-acre parcels from the widow's land holdings. Their properties surrounded our farm. They were part of the radical right, a phrase coined by Seymour Martin Lipset in 1955 to describe extremists who, among other things, hated immigrants. Greg invited me to come over to his yard through a hole in the fence between our land. We spent a few hours playing until Greg's mother saw us. She recognized me as the boy from the immigrant family who lived on the farm across the fence and angrily sent me home. Then she hit Greg as they walked back toward their house. Greg's father repaired the hole in the fence that evening. When I saw Greg again, he was afraid and said that he could not talk with me. A similar thing happened when I met another neighbor named Doug, Greg's cousin, who was my age. After his mother learned who my parents were, she sent me home and let me know in no uncertain terms that I was not welcome. There were several other children about my age who lived nearby, and their parents said unkind things about my family and forbade them from playing with me.

I recall that kids in the neighborhood called me a "Bojon." I learned that Bojon was a derogatory term used to describe immigrants of Slovenian descent who lived in Pueblo. There was only one family that allowed me to play with their son. His name was Benji, and he was a year younger than me. I never felt that Benji's parents accepted me, but only tolerated my presence because I treated their son well. The other children bullied Benji because he had a terrible scar on his face from a childhood accident. It never mattered to me if people looked different. I had learned through Mom's example to be accepting of everyone regardless of physical imperfections, different skin color, different religion, or other traits that set them apart. Mom practiced "Love thy neighbor as thyself." She instilled a sense of empathy in me. I always remember how I felt when the parents of the children I wanted to play with sent me home because I was different. I didn't have any other friends besides Benji, so I spent a lot of time with Mom when she was at home, and with my Aunt Mary.

I started kindergarten in the fall of 1958. It was difficult since I did not want to leave home and was afraid of going to school. I was the problem child that all kindergarten teachers feared. Mom walked me to school the first day, and I rebelled. She told me I needed to try school out and that if I did not like it, she would come and get me. That calmed me down, and I stopped fighting. When I got to the school, I was quiet at first while other children were crying and fussing. Since I had promised Mom, I tried to adjust. I was so good at the start that the teacher used me as an example of how others should behave. During the first two hours, I behaved well because I was curious. Then I got bored. I told the teacher that I wanted to go home. She said I couldn't. I argued that Mom had promised to pick me up if I did not like school and I made it clear that I did not. When the teacher refused to call Mom, I had a crying fit. I was stubborn, and I cried every morning during the first week. I finally settled down after making a new friend in kindergarten named Jay. Best of all, Jay's family had just moved in across the street from my Uncle Mike's house. My universe had expanded; now I had a second friend.

Things were going well for our family at the start of 1959. The farm was producing and generating income. Mom and Dad had almost paid off the bank loan for the house and their circle of friends kept growing.

Mom depended on Mary to take care of me. I worshiped Mary. My nickname for her was Auntie. One of my favorite memories is when she taught me to play checkers. She prepared peanut butter and jelly sandwiches for lunch, using jellies that she had made from her fruit and berry garden. My favorite was peanut butter and gooseberry jelly. After lunch, Auntie brought out her checkerboard and we would play. She was a fierce competitor and never went easy on me.

As I learned board strategy, I continued to improve and came closer to winning each game. The first time that I won, I could hardly believe it. Neither could Auntie. She hated losing, so when Uncle Mike returned home from work, I bragged about winning a game. Auntie was not happy. We still played every day when she took care of me, and I began to win my share of games. Eventually, I was able to win most of the time. When I got too good, we played less. She then decided to teach me card games. The first game she taught me was gin rummy. As I learned the strategy, I began to win at gin rummy consistently. Auntie then taught me how to play bridge. When I started to master bridge, she decided to invite a couple of friends from her bridge club to play. Auntie and I teamed up, to their surprise. I was nearly six years old; her friends thought she was joking and did not take the game seriously. When we won the game, it shocked them. Then they began to play seriously. Auntie took great pleasure in winning game after game. Other players from her bridge club came over to play out of curiosity, and most of the time we would win. I had never seen Auntie so pleased.

Out of the blue, Aunt Inga sent Mom money for my birthday on July 2, 1959, to purchase train tickets so that we could visit her in New Jersey. Mom was going to say no and tell Aunt Inga that she was needed at work. But Aub, her boss, would hear nothing of the sort and twisted Mom's arm into taking a paid vacation. Mom purchased the train tickets on a summer special for an August departure. There was money left over.

After obtaining the train tickets, the shit hit the fan. The United Steelworkers of America voted to strike against the nation's steel mills on July 15, 1959. It looked like we would not be visiting Aunt Inga since everyone predicted that the strike would be a long one. But Dad insisted that we go. He convinced Mom that there was enough money for the trip. In addition, Dad had the resources to pay off the mortgage using Mom's vacation pay, income from the rental property, and farm income. The remaining funds in the family savings account were sufficient to cover bills for at least a few more months. Dad's logic convinced Mom to take Ines and me on the two-week vacation.

We departed on August 3, 1959. Our first stop was in Buffalo, New York, where we visited Nickola and his wife, Anka. That was when Nickola told me about his and my father's adventures in Yugoslavia and Germany.

Then an old friend of the family from Germany who lived in Niagara Falls, Ontario, came to Buffalo to drive us to his home in Canada. We met several of my parents' friends who had migrated to Canada as displaced persons. They had made special trips to Niagara Falls from various parts of Canada just to see Mom. One of my fondest memories of Canada was driving to a beach on the Canadian side of Lake Erie and having a picnic. Mom's friends knew how much she loved the water, and they coaxed her to swim. It took a little convincing. But this was the first beach that she had been to since leaving Germany. Mom had gained weight after my birth, but the power she displayed swimming was a sight to behold. I wasn't alone in watching her with awe. She glided through the water gracefully. Her strokes were effortless and generated tremendous speed. She was so fast that the other swimmers could not keep up with her.

On the way back to the United States, we stopped to visit Niagara Falls on the Canadian side. It was a magnificent sight, which we enjoyed and talked about often. Then my dad's friend drove us to New York City to catch the train to Philadelphia, where Aunt Inga and her husband, Adolf, met us. We spent a few days visiting with them in Riverside, New Jersey. Inga had migrated to Philadelphia in 1949 as a displaced person. Uncle Valentine had sponsored her. Valentine had come from Austria just before World War I and worked alongside my grandfather Bek in the shipyards. Inga met Adolf in Philadelphia and was married in 1951. She had her daughter Franny in 1952 and a son Victor in 1954. I was sad to leave Philadelphia. I wanted to spend more time with my cousins. But we had to get back home because I was going to start first grade.

My father's best friend, Frenchie, whose given name was Art, met us at the train station. Frenchie was a nickname that was derived from his French heritage. He was as close to our family as any person could be. As mentioned earlier, he had met Dad on his first day at the steel mill and befriended him. When Dad only had a bike for transportation, Frenchie went out of his way to give him rides. Frenchie was the brother that Uncle Mike never was. He was an important part of my life during childhood. He gave me my first bike on my seventh birthday when my dad didn't have the money to buy one. Frenchie was a rotund man who stood about five feet ten inches tall. He had a round head and a drinker's nose. His face was scarred and worn from a lifetime of alcoholism, but it maintained a warmth that reflected his personality. He always had a crew cut and wore glasses. Frenchie eventually died of liver failure, when I was 11. After we returned from our vacation, I remember seeing my father in the field working, when Frenchie honked the horn. Dad dropped his hoe and ran to greet us. I had missed my father and was happy to see him.

START OF GRADE SCHOOL

I began first grade in the fall of 1959 at our parish's grade school. The first day in a new school frightened me, but I remember being overjoyed when my friend Jay from kindergarten showed up. All my other classmates from kindergarten had gone to public school. My first-grade teacher was Sister Mary David. She was a pleasant person. I remember that most of the kids could read at the start of first grade, but I could not. I was eager to learn and progressed rapidly. I found that the pace of the class was too slow, so I got bored easily. Sister Mary David misjudged my boredom as me having difficulty with the material. I didn't misbehave during class despite being bored. I tried to stay out of trouble.

Ines started tenth grade at a new high school called Pueblo South. It upset Ines that her best friend, Pat, lived in a different school district and went to Pueblo Central. Ines was an outcast at South High. The teachers were not supportive and treated her badly because she was an immigrant. There were other outcasts who were friendly toward her, though. They made South High tolerable for Ines, but she missed Pat. They often met at Central High school hangouts.

The United Steelworkers of America's strike lasted longer than anyone thought: 116 days. My mom's income as a housekeeper kept the family afloat. Fortunately, Mom and Dad had learned from their experiences during the war and understood that times could unexpectedly get lean; they were prepared for the worst. The farm kept us from going hungry. We survived on the produce that was grown, harvested, and canned. We also had chickens, rabbits, ducks, goats, and pigs. But by the time the strike ended, Mom and Dad had butchered most of the livestock except for a couple of hens and a rooster. I was young and oblivious to how dire the family's situation was. When I got past my rebellious teens and early twenties, I finally understood what my family had gone through. I never remember being afraid during these times, despite the peril we were in. I always knew that I would be protected and cared for. Looking back, I regret that I complained so much about not having new toys.

After they settled the strike, the union did well for its membership. Working conditions were much better and Dad's salary increased. He continued to work hard, both at the mill and on the farm. He continued to bring in successful crops year after year and made money. He had a comfortable life, but he still was not satisfied. The dream of making it big in America never went away. Dad spent a lot of time looking for the right business opportunity. Having paid off the home loan early, he was willing to take another risk. The right opportunity fell into his lap after the strike ended. A friend's father needed to raise money and was looking to sell 100 acres of land about a mile outside of Aspen, Colorado. Dad and his friend drove to Aspen to look at the property. With his background in skiing, Dad recognized the potential of this property. Aspen reminded him of the successful ski resorts he knew in Europe. It was poised to grow, and this piece of land was in the right spot. His friend's father was willing to sell the land to my father for $8,000. Dad went to the bank seeking a loan but was refused unless my Uncle Mike was willing to co-sign. Uncle Mike again rejected co-signing the loan despite my dad's logical arguments about the value of the property. He told Mike that it would be worth millions in ten years. He offered to share the profits. But my uncle would not hear of it. He did not trust my father's judgment. This was a tremendous disappointment to Dad because he believed this was his best opportunity to be successful since he arrived in the United States. The land was sold to a developer about a month later. Afterward, hard feelings continued to linger between Dad and Uncle Mike. My father followed the meteoric rise of land prices in Aspen, and each year he would become angrier.

Mom worked herself to the bone as a housekeeper and cook, but she still found time to do charitable work in the parish soup kitchen and always gravitated toward helping others. Mom's personality was magical. She was an extrovert who could have in-depth conversations with anyone. The poor who went to the soup kitchen were in desperate need of someone who cared and valued them. Mom thrived on making them feel good about themselves. In return, they loved her.

Dad worked hard at the mill. He took any overtime that he could get. Dad was sending money to Yugoslavia to care for his extended family, and he continued to dream about starting a business. He would come home after a 16-hour shift, lie down, and fall into a deep sleep. When he woke up, he would do some chores around the farm and then get ready for his next shift at the mill. He had minor injuries from the demanding labor at the mill, like sprains and burns. But he would go to work anyway. Even a cold or flu would not stop him.

Uncle Mike retired in the fall of 1959. He and Auntie spent a lot of their time fishing and camping. One sunny weekend in early November, they invited me to tag along on a fishing trip. It was a warm Saturday, and the lake was close by. They convinced Mom to let me go. I used a spare rod and reel. They taught me how to bait the hook and cast the line. I did very well and demonstrated a knack for fishing. For Christmas, Uncle Mike gave me a Zebco rod and reel starter set. He also bought himself a pink Cadillac as a retirement splurge. The car was impressive. It had electric seats, electric windows, an oncoming headlight detector, and many more amenities. The oncoming headlight detector was a perfect safety feature for driving on narrow mountain roads at night to get to the lake before the fish started biting at daylight. A person could drive with the bright lights on for excellent visibility around hairpin curves. The car would then detect oncoming traffic and automatically dim the lights.

I went with my aunt and uncle on several fishing trips during the spring and summer of 1960. It was not long before I became proficient at the sport. Our trips were a lot of fun. I remember one trip in the summer of 1960 that was particularly exciting. We were at Lake DeWeese near Westcliffe, Colorado, and started fishing before other anglers had arrived. Uncle Mike had a secret bait that he wanted to try, raw liver chunks covered with garlic powder. At 9:30 a.m. he had a bite. After setting the hook, it took him an hour to reel in the fish. By then it had tangled up every fishing line around us. The fish turned out to be a nine-pound German brown trout. It was about an ounce off the state record at the time. When we got home that evening, Dad came out to the car when I was being dropped off. Uncle Mike opened the car's trunk and showed him the giant fish in the cooler. Mom appeared to see what the commotion was about. She looked at the fish and gagged. She hurried away. I asked Mom about it later and that is when I found out that her revulsion to fish was due to the rotted fish oil that they gave her as rations when she was a slave laborer in Germany. I finally understood why she refused to prepare fish back in the day when the Catholic Church imposed meatless Fridays. She found it difficult to be in the same room when fish was being prepared and served.

I started second grade in 1960. The class was taught by a very sweet lay teacher, Miss Bea. But this was her first job. The kids took advantage of her and she could not control the class. This was a wild school year. My friend Jay enjoyed the chaos in the classroom but, at first, I had a hard time adjusting. Mom had conditioned me to be a gentleman. I tried to sit quietly while the classroom erupted around me. Jay urged me to join in, but I didn't want to. Eventually, he began ignoring me and made friends with Jim, who relished being mischievous. Jay no longer wanted to be around me. I remember when the switch turned on and I had to decide between losing one of my few friends while trying to behave or joining in on the mischief and keeping my best friend. I joined in. It was a life-changing choice. Jay and I became the two biggest troublemakers in the second-grade class.

1960 was an important year for Mom because I had my first communion. She was so proud. My parents' hospitality was famous. Food, drink, and music were a vital part of their get-togethers. Friends loved to come over just for the experience. Mom would always have baked goods in the house and people coveted her delicacies. The various pastries that she baked were better than any I have tasted in my world travels since. Mom tinkered with old family recipes and perfected them. Dad had nonstop refills of wine and beer for his guests. Celebrations like New Year's Eve, Thanksgiving, and Christmas were so special that people would come over uninvited. Mom and Dad turned no one away. All the family friends knew that my first communion was going to be a celebration beyond compare and they showed up in droves.

The other memorable event that occurred during my second-grade year was in May 1961. The high school principal gave Ines permission to leave class in the morning to take her citizenship test at the courthouse. In the middle of her American history class, she raised her hand. The teacher had been notified that Ines would have to leave class that day and, through gossip from the principal's staff, had learned the reason. He excused my sister. After she departed, he then informed the class why she left and made fun of her. My sister learned about the teacher's inexcusable behavior that night from one of her classmates. My sister passed the test and took the citizenship oath. It was an extremely exciting day for her. Even the actions of a rude and irresponsible teacher couldn't spoil Ines's day.

After second grade, I stayed with Auntie during the summer while Mom worked. One day in late June, Aunt Mary urgently needed to see her sister, Frances Keš. Frances lived in Denver, and Auntie had to take me along. Frances was married to the attorney and chief financial officer for the Croatian Fraternal Union of America, Tony Keš. When we drove up to the Keš mansion in Wheat Ridge, Colorado, Frances was waiting outside. Frances was a woman who always tried to look regal but fell short. She wore a black dress and was made up like a porcelain doll. She had her dyed platinum-blond hair in a bun. Frances scowled pointing at me. "Why did you bring him?" Her sister's comment shocked Auntie. Frances continued, "He is not allowed in my house and must stay in the car."

Auntie walked indignantly into the house and I could hear them arguing. I heard Frances speak rather loudly. "Why did you bring that white trash with you?" Frances was watching her grandchildren that day, a girl named Jane, who was about my age; and a boy named David, who was about a year younger. Eventually, her grandchildren exited the house to get away from the fighting. They noticed me in the car and walked up to the window. I was told by Jane that I could not go into the house, but she thought it was all right for me to be outside with them. I got out of the car and we played together. We had fun until Frances saw me with her grandchildren. She then stormed out of the house and hit me. She heatedly said, "I told you to stay in the car." Auntie rushed out and was furious with her. The two of them went back inside and argued. The fight became physical. Jane panicked and called her grandfather to come home right away. He worked a few blocks away and arrived within minutes. Tony entered the house to see what the fray between the sisters was about. Twenty minutes later, he came out of the house and apologized to me. Then he invited me in. He showed me around the house and prepared some snacks and soft drinks for his grandchildren and me. He then went back into his home office, where Auntie and Frances sat silently waiting, and then shut the door. I could hear their muffled voices. After about 15 minutes, Frances came out with Tony and Auntie and apologized indifferently to me. Tony told us we could go play in the game room. Auntie spent another two hours with Frances talking. As we drove home, I was curious and asked Auntie, "Why did Frances call me white trash?"

"Frances is full of herself," she said. Then she paused and looked at me. "Never take nasty comments from vile people seriously."

When I returned home from Denver, I told Mom what Frances had done. Mom explained to me that Frances thought everyone was beneath her. She rationalized that there are many people in the world like Frances, and I shouldn't get angry with all of them. Otherwise, I would go through life as a very angry person. Rather, I should feel sorry for them. Mom confided that these types of people end up with no friends or loved ones. Twenty years later, my mom and Uncle Mike went to visit Frances and Tony in Denver. By then, Tony was suffering from Alzheimer's. Frances grieved about her fate, telling Uncle Mike, "Tony was once the smartest person in the world and now look at him." Tony did not know who Frances was, but he remembered Uncle Mike and was lucid while talking to him. Tony and Frances had two boys, Ted and John. Ted had children and John committed suicide. John was a gentle soul who was forced into marriage by his domineering mother. My mom was sad for him because she believed he was gay and had to hide that part of himself from the world. Before Mike left, Frances lamented that her children and grandchildren had abandoned her. Mom was right; in the end Frances was alone, without family and friends.

Third grade began in the fall of 1961. Jay and I were rebels racing into the eye of a terrible storm. Our teacher, Sister Antonia Michael, wore the traditional penguin suit that concealed all but her face. She was not unattractive. But looks can deceive; she was sadistic. The nun immediately took a dislike to us. The entire year was a never-ending series of nightmares. One incident had a profound effect on me and stood out above all the other horrors that occurred during that year. Sister Antonia Michael had a perverse way of getting rid of problem boys from her class. At the time, I was too young to understand why the nuns in the school kept the priest away from the children. Sister Antonia Michael broke this unspoken rule when dealing with boys she disliked. She sent them to the rectory for punishment. I knew of boys whom she sent to the rectory who never came back to class. I could have had the same fate, but an older friend gave me a dire warning: "Don't you ever go into the rectory." Sister Antonia Michael ordered me to the rectory one day out of spite. As I walked toward the building, I saw that she went back into the schoolhouse when I was halfway there. I then turned right rather than left and headed for Pueblo City Park, which was about halfway to my house. I spent the rest of the day at the playground. When I made it home, I thought that someone would call my parents to tell them I played hooky. I expected to be expelled or disciplined. However, the call never came. I then worried that the nun would punish me when I came to class the next morning. Instead, she seemed surprised to see me but said nothing. It struck me like lightning that the priest and the nuns were not talking to each other. From then on, every time Sister Antonia Michael sent me to the rectory, I played hooky.

Eventually, angry parents confronted Sister Louise Michael, the school principal, about Sister Antonia Michael. The principal immediately stopped her from sending boys to the rectory. By then, four boys who had been sent to the rectory by Sister Antonia Michael had been taken out of the school by their parents. What happened in the rectory was never openly spoken about. I can only surmise what transpired.

I regret putting Mom through the constant visits with the principal during third grade. But she was a wonderful parent; she defended me. Her position was that I was not being challenged by the lessons. She also taught me how to handle disagreeable people and not to give in to my worst compulsions. She assured me she understood how I felt about having a terrible teacher. It was during one of these discussions that she told me the story about her grade-school teacher hitting her and how she learned to swim from observing frogs.

By 1962, my uncle's old nemesis, Tony Sraka, took advantage of the brewing feud between my father and uncle. Sraka used my father to get back at Uncle Mike. He befriended Dad and offered to help him start a business. Sraka was a true con man. My dad was wonderful at reading people, but Sraka was so slick that Dad did not see that he was being scammed. He gave Sraka the reverence one would bestow on a Mafia godfather. He often visited his white three-story Gothic home in the middle of Pueblo. He took gifts of wine and smoked meat. By 1962, Sraka had become a fat, disgusting, bald old man with rotten teeth who spit when he talked. I had the misfortune of being dragged along on one of my father's visits. Sraka preached and my father listened intently. About an hour into the visit, a young woman, who looked like she was barely 16, walked down a stairway that was visible from the kitchen where we sat. Sraka ordered her to come in and my dad watched in awe. He asked her to get my dad a drink. Even though I was nine years old, I could see that Sraka had staged this for my father's benefit. As a skilled grifter, Sraka recognized my dad's weaknesses and exploited them. After we got home, I told Mom that we had visited Sraka. Mom was angry at Dad. She chewed him out; he sat quietly and took it. Mom detested Sraka because of an incident that had occurred the year before. Sraka had requested that Dad send Mom over to interpret a letter he had received from Yugoslavia. My sister drove Mom to his house. Once inside his home, they discovered that Sraka did not need an interpreter. The request was a pretext to lure my mom into his house. He tried to sexually assault both my mom and my sister. That Sraka was able to convince my father that this assault was a simple misunderstanding showed his prowess as a grifter.

Tony Sraka made sure that Mike was aware of his friendship with my father. Uncle Mike tried to warn Dad he was dangerous. But Dad blew up, telling his brother that Sraka was going to help him with his business ideas. Dad reminded Mike that he had lost out on the business opportunity of a lifetime because of Mike's unwillingness to co-sign for a loan. After that vicious argument, Uncle Mike and Aunt Mary wanted nothing to do with our family. About a year later, Dad figured out that Sraka never kept his promises and he stopped visiting him.

That rift meant that Aunt Mary quit babysitting me. Mom couldn't find anyone else to care for me while she worked. But I convinced her I could care for myself. I showed her how Auntie had taught me to make sandwiches, fry eggs, fry bacon, fry steaks, boil Chef Boyardee spaghetti in a pot, make pancakes, fry spam, etc. Mom reluctantly left me alone for a trial run. She eventually developed confidence in my abilities to be on my own.

In 1963, Arlen and Larry were getting older, and Mom felt that it was time to move on. Dr. Trent, one of Aub's friends, offered Mom a job in health care. She took the offer. Aub and Harriet dearly loved Mom and were heartbroken to see her leave. Mom remained close to them and their children for the rest of her life. That was typical. No friend ever wanted to drift apart from her.

I can't put my finger on what made her so charismatic. One thing that stood out was her unconditional acceptance of people regardless of their deficiencies. That is a rare trait. Remarkably, Mom never said anything negative about another person no matter how mean-spirited they were. The only exception I recall was Tony Sraka. She had a moral compass so powerful that it rubbed off on people close to her. Mom's personality had saved her life and the lives of others more than once during the war. I have met no one like her, and I don't think I ever will.

Mom had had a strong desire to work in medicine since childhood. Dr. Trent needed an aide to take care of his mother-in-law, Mrs. Young, who was a patient at Sharmar Nursing Home. Dr. Trent also encouraged Mom to become a licensed practical nurse. She took his advice and worked hard to qualify. After receiving the license, Mom was ecstatic. She had finally achieved her lifelong goal at the age of 41.

In 1963, I started fourth grade and was very responsible for my age. Fourth grade was mostly uneventful but, occasionally, Sister Antonia Michael would substitute for my fourth-grade teacher, Mrs. Holland.

Whenever Sister Antonia Michael substituted, it was a bad day. But Mrs. Holland was a beloved teacher who had retired from the public schools and had continued teaching in Catholic schools. After seeing what a professional teacher could do, I begged my parents to send me to public school. I argued that Catholic schools did not require their teachers to have state certification. The nuns who taught at my school certainly didn't. Most had never even taken a college course. A lot of them were in their seventies, so this was not unusual. I knew of one sister who had been on the *Titanic* as a 37-year-old woman. Her promise to God was that she would become a nun; she was still teaching at 88.

My reasoning did no good; Mom wanted me to share her devotion to religion. She believed that an education in a Catholic school would help me find God in my life. Plus, she believed that Catholic schools were academically better than public schools. My parents would not even listen to my criticisms.

I think it was during fourth grade that I finally proved to Mom that I could handle any emergency. One day after school, I walked home rather than wait for a bus. At the corner of Prairie and Goodnight, as I was crossing the street, a new Buick stopped in front of me. In the car, there was a well-dressed lady about my mom's age wearing a stylish hat and a man wearing a suit who was driving. I remember that the man had a hat on as well. They both looked out of place and, even at that young age, I sensed they were trying too hard to look respectable. The lady called out to me, "Your mom asked me to pick you up."

I did not recognize her. "What is my mom's name?" I asked.

The lady responded, "I don't remember."

I immediately saw through the lie. There were many people around the area since school was getting out, so I felt safe that this couple would not try to force me into the car. I continued to walk. As I made my way along Goodnight toward home, the car followed me. When I reached a Protestant church two blocks away, I turned and ran into the church. The pastor was there and saw me. "What is wrong?" he asked.

I told him, "A strange lady and a man in a Buick are following me."

He went outside where the car was waiting. The pastor scared them away. "Can I call your parents?" he asked.

"They are at work," I said. He invited me to stay with him and said that he would find someone to give me a ride home. I told him I had a friend who lived a block away and I would go there. He reluctantly let me leave and walked with me to make sure that the car had gone. When we got to my friend's house, he knocked on the door and watched me go in. I stayed for about ten minutes and left. Rather than walk along Goodnight to get through the city park, I took a different route. I kept to a large, wooded expanse in the middle of the park, far away from any road. I glimpsed the Buick in the distance driving along Goodnight, but the occupants did not see me. I ran from tree to tree to hide and to watch for the car. Eventually, I reached the swimming pool on the other side of the park and ran across the empty field between the pool and Park Drive. I did not see the Buick. Our driveway was close by, so I ran to my house and locked the doors. I sat with our dog, Fury, a German shepherd-collie mix who would bark if she heard a car coming down our driveway. I also knew that Fury would protect me. Thankfully, no car appeared. When Mom got home, I was happy to see her. I told her what had happened. Mom called the church and talked to the pastor, thanking him for helping.

The incident upset Mom, but she said, "You did the right thing." I did not tell her the rest of the story about the Buick looking for me in the park. I was afraid that she would not trust me to be alone anymore. About a week later, I went to the mailbox at the end of our driveway. The same two people in the Buick were driving along Park Drive and saw me. They tried to pick me up again. I ran to the widow's old house, where a family of six had moved in a few years back. I knocked on the door. The mom, named Pat, answered the door and I pointed at the people in the car watching me and told her they were trying to pick me up. She grabbed a nearby shotgun and walked toward the car. The driver screeched the tires as the car raced away. Pat walked me home and told Mom what had happened. Pat promised Mom that she would watch for strangers and that I could go to her place anytime.

The strangers never came back. However, there was a story in the newspaper a week later about a boy around my age who had disappeared near the Mineral Palace park on the other side of the city. Mom started trusting my judgment and my ability to handle emergencies. From then on, she knew that she did not have to worry about me.

I missed Auntie terribly and walked over to her house every month to visit. She would scold me, saying that I shouldn't be there, but she obviously missed me as well and would invite me in. Auntie asked me not to tell my mom I had been there. I missed the fishing trips with Uncle Mike and Auntie. I begged my dad to take me fishing, but he had no interest because of the experiences he had had on fishing boats. A family friend, Charlie, took pity on me and invited me on one of his fishing trips in the spring of 1963. After Charlie saw that I was a serious angler, he invited me to go on other trips that year. I think Dad became a little jealous of my close relationship with Charlie. Charlie didn't have a son. On July 4, 1963, Dad took me on a camping trip to San Isabel Lake with Frenchie. I fished while Dad and Frenchie polished off the beer and wine they had brought along. Dad enjoyed the camping trip; then we began to camp more often. During these trips, Dad eventually figured out that fishing in Colorado was fun. It was nothing like the fishing he had known from the commercial boats and trawlers. Dad was not only a lucky angler —he would catch fish when no one else was getting bites—but he was skilled as well. We began taking regular fishing trips with his other close friends until I turned 14. I then lost interest and stopped going. Dad was heartbroken, but fishing remained an important part of his life.

During one of my outings to Uncle Mike's house in the fall of 1963, Mary's son Leonard and his family were visiting. It was the first time Leonard had seen Mary since her divorce from his father. Auntie was nervous because this was intended to be a reconciliation visit. Leonard's father had passed away in 1952 and his children had never met their grandmother. Aunt Mary was glad to see me. She asked me to keep Leonard's two daughters company while she and Leonard talked privately. We went outside, and I introduced them to my best friend, Jay, and his two sisters, who lived across the street. I kept them occupied, and they had fun with Jay's sisters. After a couple of hours, Leonard and his wife, Amy, were ready to drive back to Boulder. They thanked me for making sure that their girls were not alone. I could see that Leonard's visit made Auntie happy. Being able to see her grandchildren was a dream come true.

Our family experienced a major crisis in the spring of 1963—a free-swinging hook block hanging off a ceiling crane struck Dad at the mill. The operator had failed to bring up the cable when he moved the crane from one end of the mill to the other. He did not watch for workers on the floor, and the block almost hit several other people. My father could not completely get out of its path and took a glancing blow on his back. It pushed him off the platform he was standing on and he fell about 15 feet and broke his leg. The nurse in the mill infirmary called Mom and told her that Dad had been in an accident. He requested that she come. Mom found a ride, and I insisted on going along. Dad was being prepped to leave by ambulance. The nurse told Mom that he was fine. He had a broken femur and a broken rib. She said that he was a little nervous when they removed his clothing. At the hospital, they put him in an orthopedic cast that went up to his hip. He had to wear the cast for three months during the summer and was on crutches. He was miserable. When they removed the cast, it took another month for him to walk normally. He went back to work after four months and met with his supervisor. The accident report that the supervisor had filed had blamed my father for the accident and had covered up for the careless operator, who was the supervisor's cousin. The foreperson brought my father into his office and accused him of causing the accident and then fired him. Several of the workers who had witnessed the accident accompanied my father to union headquarters and told the union representative the true story. After hearing the facts behind the accident, the union representative demanded an immediate meeting with the president of Colorado Fuel and Iron. The union representative prepared affidavits about the accident and had the witnesses sign them. He was aware of the crane operator. It wasn't the first time that this operator had been careless. The representative had already been preparing a file on him that was full of complaints from mill workers about his incompetence and carelessness and the injuries that he had caused. In the file there was evidence that the crane operator was the supervisor's cousin. The representative showed the president the affidavits plus the contents of the file. He told the president that the union would go on strike if he did not reinstate my father and do something about the crane operator. After reading the affidavits and the file, the president reinstated my father. The president then brought the supervisor and the crane operator into his office and fired them on the spot. To this day, I am thankful that the union protected my father from an abusive manager. They saved our family.

1963 was significant for Ines as well because she graduated from high school. Uncle Mike kept a promise that he had made to Ines when she was young that he would pay for her college. He ended up covering her tuition to attend Southern Colorado State College in the fall of 1963. Ines spent a semester in college but quit to find a job. She worked in various positions until 1969, when she settled on a career in banking. Ines started as a bank teller at Midway Bank. Her work impressed the bank president, and she was promoted to loan officer in 1976. In 1978, there was an armed robbery. Ines kept a cool head while those around her panicked, and she had the courage to alert the police during the robbery. They gave Ines an award for her actions. The banking industry floundered in 1979 when the Federal Reserve raised its discount rate to 12 percent because of inflation. Midway Bank continued to struggle until 1982, when auditors found that its president had embezzled funds. The bank closed its doors, which forced Ines to find an alternative career path.

In 1963, I went through the sacrament of Confirmation in the Roman Catholic Church, even though I knew I would not stay in the Church. My mother wanted me to be confirmed, and I would not disappoint her. It was also the year I learned about Mom's injury during the bombing of Hamburg, which she revealed after I played a prank on my sister. The prank came about because I had remembered a story Mom had told me while she was working as a housekeeper for Aub and Harriet and their sons Arlen and Larry. Larry had played a joke on Arlen. He made a banana split for his brother but replaced the whipped cream with shaving cream. Mom told me that he sprinkled on nuts, drizzled on some chocolate syrup, and put a cherry on top. She said it looked good, and Arlen fell for the prank hook, line, and sinker by putting a big spoonful in his mouth.

The story made me laugh, and I wanted badly to play that same prank someday. It took a few years for an opportunity to present itself. On that day in 1963, I was angry at my sister for devouring some cherries I had picked that day. In revenge, I asked her if she wanted me to make a banana split with freshly picked cherries on top, and she said that it sounded good. So, I made a banana split exactly like the one that Mom had described. It looked so good after I put on the finishing touches that it tempted me to take a spoonful. I then called Ines and, after she acknowledged me, I waited patiently in the next room. She did not show up after ten minutes, so I called again, telling her that the banana split was melting. She responded that she would be there soon. After a few minutes, I heard the clinking of a spoon on the bowl and I expected an immediate response. But that did not occur. I then walked into the kitchen and saw Mom finishing the last bite of the banana split. I couldn't believe my eyes. "Mom, that was for Ines," I yelled.

She answered, "It was melting and didn't want to waste it."

"Couldn't you taste the shaving cream?" I asked.

"Oh, my God," Mom responded.

She then told me she had lost her ability to taste and smell as a result of the shrapnel that had hit her during the bombing of Hamburg. Mom said she ate the banana split because she enjoyed the texture of whipped cream and the cold of ice cream. I worried about her getting sick and did not sleep that night. Fortunately, she was fine the next day.

A TIME OF CHANGE

In 1964, a series of events began that changed our lives. Perhaps the worst occurred on March 9, when birds began pecking at my mom's bedroom window at 10 p.m. The same thing had occurred when Grandma Jana died, and the event upset Mom. Within an hour, the phone rang and woke her up. Uncle Mike told her that Aunt Mary had had a stroke and was in a coma. The doctors did not expect her to live much longer, and Mike wanted us to say our goodbyes. At that moment, the feud between my uncle and father was forgotten. My parents raced Ines and me to the hospital. We rushed up to the floor that Auntie was on, but a nurse stopped me. The hospital rules were strict about not allowing anyone under 14 to visit a patient. My parents begged the nurse to let me pass because my aunt was dying and we needed to see her, but the nurse did not budge. She placed me in a waiting room where I sat alone and cried. Auntie was as close to me as Mom. I did not get to see her before she died at 1 a.m. on March 10.

When my parents and Ines entered the hospital room, they reported that Uncle Mike was holding Auntie's hand. Frances, her sister, was sitting in a chair intently watching. Frances had been in Colorado Springs visiting her brother, Johnny, when Mike called to deliver the bad news. Frances immediately left Johnny's house and made the 35-minute trip to Pueblo. Her presence surprised Mom because Frances never went out of her way for anything or anybody. Seeing how distraught Mike was, Mom asked if he had eaten anything. He shook his head no. "Come with us and we will get you a sandwich and some coffee," said Mom. His movements were slow and measured. Then Mike stood up and followed Mom and Dad to the end of the hall, where there were sandwiches and refreshments. Ines remained in the room with Frances. Ines moved to Auntie's side, weeping, and held her hand. Frances stood up and looked out the door. She then walked to Auntie's left side and reached down to grab Auntie's rings. She tugged to get them off Auntie's finger and, shocked by this, Ines glared. "What are you doing?" asked Ines. "Leave her rings alone."

Frances snarled. "She is going to die; I am taking the rings." Ines tried to stop her, but Frances pulled them off, put them in her purse, and rushed out of the door, leaving my sister behind, screaming, "Bring them back!"

When my parents returned with Mike, they could see how upset Ines was. She told them what Frances had done. Realizing that there was nothing she could do about Frances, Mom comforted her daughter. Mike and Dad were dumbfounded.

Auntie's funeral was difficult for me. She was the first person I was close to who had died. Seeing her in the casket tore me up inside. I was in shock and unable to let my emotions out. I got through the rest of the school year, but I wasn't the same person. I suffered through nightmares, anxiety, and loss of concentration. Mom and Dad had seen so many people die during the war that they could cope with Auntie's death. I know it affected Ines because I could hear her cry in her room at night for a time. Without Auntie, Uncle Mike was a lost soul. At first, he came over for dinner and spent time with the family. Eventually, he drifted away. We did not see him for months at a time. He took frequent trips. About a year later, he met a woman 20 years younger than himself. After a short romance, Uncle Mike married her. When my father and mother met Uncle Mike's new wife, Ruth, they both could see that she was a gold digger. Ruth spent Uncle Mike's life savings quickly. When the money ran out a year and a half later, so did Ruth. Uncle Mike was alone, destitute, and drinking heavily. His only income was from his pension and social security. He did not have enough money to pay his bills and taxes. Mom and Dad rescued him by paying them. Mom sat down with Uncle Mike and went through his finances. Mom discovered that he didn't know how to handle money. Auntie had always taken care of that for him. Mom realized that Mike was in serious trouble. She convinced Mike to downsize by selling his house and land on Westwood Lane. Uncle Mike bought a newly built cookie-cutter house in the Sunset Boulevard area with half of the money from the sale of his home. Mom then paid off his remaining bills and set up a savings account for emergencies with the rest. Mom put Uncle Mike on a strict budget and forced him to live within his means. Mom continued to help Uncle Mike by taking care of his money, and cooking and cleaning for him. Life went on and we acclimated to not having Aunite in our lives.

Another significant change occurred in the spring of 1965, when the sixth-graders in my class took an IQ test. When the results came back, the nuns thought that I had cheated. They forced me to take a second test with a person in the room watching closely. I scored even higher on the second test. The nuns couldn't believe the results; they had always thought that I was slow. The nuns were so bad at teaching that I was constantly bored. The principal, Sister Louise Michael, talked to Mom and told her that my score was the highest that she had ever seen. She instructed Mom not to tell me what my IQ was. But I overheard Mom talking to Dad about it that night. Mom assured Dad that I would do well in school whenever I decided to. Dad was proud and responded, "My boy."

An event that had an enormous impact on me also occurred in the fall of 1965, when Ines drove me to the Sharmar Nursing Home, where Mom worked. While I was there, one nurse came in and asked Mom for help. Mom made sure that an aide stayed with her patient, Mrs. Young, and left to help. Ines and I talked with Mrs. Young. She was so happy to have visitors she talked up a storm and didn't even notice that Mom had gone. When Mom came back, it was time for Mrs. Young's bath. Ines then took me around the nursing home to visit some other patients. The sight of a 16-year-old girl who had had an anoxic brain injury from an automobile accident affected me. She was excited to see us. Her parents had abandoned her in the nursing home and, sadly, she never had visitors. I was afraid because I had never been around someone with a brain injury. Ines kept urging me to talk to her. I could see in her eyes she was excited to have guests. So, I began talking. Her happiness by that gesture was infectious. She could not talk but tried. All that came out of her mouth were grunts. She bounced up and down in her wheelchair with glee. I couldn't help but feel that life was so unfair to her. It made me realize that anyone could be struck down by a tragedy and, given all the close calls my parents had been through, how lucky I was to be alive.

Ines became a focal point for my mom in 1965. My parents pressured her to get married. It is my belief that Ines never desired marriage because our father had been so domineering—when I later asked her if that was true, she said yes. Mom took matters into her own hands. She read the classified section in a Croatian newspaper that Dad subscribed to, where young men put in ads seeking pen pals and wives. Mom found one intriguing ad. A young Croatian farmer named Zoran from Ontario, Canada, was interested in finding a Croatian wife. Mom began corresponding with him, using my sister's name. They exchanged weekly letters, and it soon became obvious that Zoran was falling in love. He had booked a trip to Pueblo, Colorado, to meet the love of his life. Mom tried to dissuade him but couldn't. She then had to break the news to my sister that a young man from Canada was coming to Pueblo to propose to her. I don't think I have ever seen my sister so angry. She told Mom to marry him herself and said that she would not be in Pueblo when he visited. Mom tried to persuade her to at least meet him. After her anger subsided, Ines reluctantly agreed to meet him if Mom would tell Zoran the truth, which she did. Zoran still wanted to meet Ines. He came to Pueblo and pleasantly surprised Ines. Zoran was a tall, well-built man who was ruggedly handsome. He spent a week with my sister, and Zoran was smitten with Ines. At the end of the week, he proposed. Ines did some soul searching but eventually refused. Zoran left heartbroken. Mom learned a valuable lesson about interfering with the lives of her children.

In the meantime, I kept pressing my parents to send me to public school because I wanted better teachers. They kept me in Catholic school because I was a bit wild, and they thought attending a Catholic school would give me a moral compass. In 1965, I started seventh grade. My teacher, Mrs. Sullivan, was a lay teacher who had spent years in the public-school system, retired, and then began teaching at my school. She was the best teacher I had up to that point. At the end of October, she had a stroke and never returned. The nuns were desperate for a replacement and gave the job to the school football and basketball coach, Mr. Guso. He told us he had a degree from the University of Nevada at Reno, where he had played running back on the football team. But everyone realized that he probably never attended class. He was not capable of teaching seventh grade. The year was a complete disaster.

Mrs. Young, Mom's patient, passed away in 1966. Mom was with her, comforting her until the last breath. Sharmar then offered Mom a job on its staff as an LPN. It was important to Mom to remain in health care. Plus, she had more nursing opportunities as a Sharmar staff member. Mom accepted the job. Most of the patients at Sharmar were put there to die alone, but my mom made sure that they were loved. In return, her patients adored her.

The nursing home wasn't too far from my grade school. So, occasionally I walked to Sharmar to visit Mom after school and make rounds with her. It was magical to watch how she interacted with these lonely, dejected people and made them feel wanted again. My mom glowed while caring for them. I could tell that nursing was her calling. She sat with many dying patients at Sharmar, comforting them as they faded away. I can't imagine how difficult that must have been for her.

Aunt Theresa, who was now living in our small rental house with Uncle Phillip, was looking for work in the summer of 1966. Mom talked to her boss at Sharmar and found a job for Aunt Theresa. It made life easier for Mom. She could ride to and from work with Aunt Theresa.

I started eighth grade in 1966; they split our courses among three teachers. Sister Ann Michael taught math, and she was even more sadistic than my third-grade teacher. Sister Davina Mary, the school principal, taught English and history. She was a nice person but not a competent teacher. The science instructor, Mr. Fas, was a layperson who was a physics student at Southern Colorado State College. He was incompetent and a terrible teacher. Most of that year, I was in survival mode and had no desire to pay attention in class. My academic performance suffered.

One day, Sister Ann Michael walked into the room and complained about the overall class performance on an exam. She then went into a tirade about an unnamed person in the class who was a genius but who had done poorly. There was no question that she was talking about me because of her occasional glances directly at me. Obviously, she had looked at my file. She ranted and raved for the entire hour. At the end of eighth grade, I was happy to leave the parish grade school. I begged my parents to send me to public school for ninth grade. But, once again, they prevailed. They enrolled me at the all-male Catholic high school, which was run by the Marianists.

HIGH SCHOOL

I started ninth grade in 1967. The Catholic high school used a poorly designed tracking system. There were three tracks: A, B and C, each with its own curriculum. Track A was for students who would go on to college. Track B was for students who would go to work after high school. The expectation for Track C was for students to fill a seat and occupy time. When the school made a placement mistake, which was frequently, it was almost impossible for a student to move up to a higher track and still graduate on time. They placed me in Track B based on the recommendation from the nuns at my grade school. I realized that I needed to dig myself out of this hole or I would never make it to college, which was important to me.

As a child, I had dreamed about going to college. I couldn't get enough of science, especially after seeing my first Sears catalog at eight. I didn't ask my parents for the type of toys that other boys my age wanted. Instead, I coveted the chemistry sets, microscopes, telescopes, and the various build-your-own science project kits. My ambition, even at eight, was to become a research scientist. Mom and Dad recognized this and strongly encouraged my interest in science by giving me chemistry sets and scientific instruments for Christmas or birthdays.

So I buckled down and focused on school in the ninth grade. I worked hard. But the tracking system barriers were almost too high. The system was so biased that the teachers used unwritten grading policies for each track. The best grade a Track B student could get was 85 percent. My school graded by percentages. You had to feel sorry for the students in Track C, because the best score they could get was 80 percent. Being in Track A was a position of privilege; the lowest score was 90 percent. The instructors graded tests downward even if a student had a perfect paper to keep the score within the track's unspoken grading policy. I made the honor roll with honors every semester for my first two years. To achieve honors, you had to have an average between 85 and 88. To get high honors, your average had to be between 89 and 93. Highest honors required an average above 93. I kept asking the principal to allow me to take Track A coursework, as did Mom. In my junior year, they finally allowed me to move to Track A. I can see how students can easily get discouraged. Even being as driven as I was, so many things could have derailed me. I was lucky to have parents who valued education and found the time to fight for me despite being pushed to exhaustion by the hard work of keeping food on the table and paying the bills. We were a poor family who lived on the margins.

There were plenty of bumps in high school, but writing about them requires a separate book. One that deserves mention here is Brother Bill. His first teaching job was in my high school. Brother Bill eventually became the subject of a series of class-action lawsuits against the Catholic Church around 2007. It made the national news because of the sheer magnitude of his pedophilia, which spanned three decades. The lawsuits involved at least 52 victims during his time in Pueblo in the 1960s, St. Louis in the 1970s, and San Antonio in the 1980s. The nature of Brother Bill's atrocities was horrific. He would tell his victims he was completing a master's thesis in psychology and asked vulnerable kids to help him with his research. The newspaper reported that he took his victims to the band room and blindfolded them before assaulting them. During my sophomore year, I learned from a friend that Brother Bill had lured him to the band room and used chloroform to render him unconscious. I believed that something unspeakable was happening to my friend. I confronted Brother Bill. He punched me in the face and broke my nose and glasses. When I went home, Mom asked me what happened. I told her who hit me and why. She then talked to the school principal, who spun a completely different story and accused me of lying. The principal had to have known what was going on, but he covered it up. What makes me even more angry now is that the 2007 court case revealed that the Marianists knew about Brother Bill's inappropriate behavior with students even before he took his vows. Mom's nature was to believe in the good of all people. She always trusted the clergy. She believed that my friend had misled me and the principal, who said the punch was accidental. I begged Mom and Dad to send me to public school, but they kept me in the Catholic high school. I made it through the gauntlet. Even though I had better teachers in high school than grade school, the teachers there still did not require state certification. Unlike the public schools, my high school did not teach advanced placement classes or calculus, which left me at a disadvantage as I prepared to apply to colleges. Yet, I was one of the first freshmen in my class to receive a varsity letter, in track and field. Academically, I continued to climb in the rankings. I made highest honors every semester during my last two years, and had the grades to apply to good colleges.

I submitted applications to several universities in 1971. My parents wanted me to go to a Catholic university. I wanted to study chemistry and physics; so, to appease my parents, I applied to a few Catholic universities that had good science programs as well as to the major state universities that had excellent science programs. All the universities I applied to accepted me, but the choice came down to the University of Colorado and Colorado State University. Colorado State University was my preference because of the lower cost. I had a limited budget. I had a scholarship from the Western Star Lodge (a Lodge in which my father was a member), which paid for my books and tuition for a couple of years, and I saved some money working over the summer. In college, I also earned money doing odd jobs such as piano moving. Dad made up the difference.

COLLEGE

After l left for college, Mom continued working at Sharmar for a few more years until her boss quit and opened a new nursing home near our house on Park Drive called Shady Rest. He begged Mom to come work for him there. She accepted the offer so as to be closer to home. Mom remained at Shady Rest for two more years.

In 1973, Uncle Mike had lost his leg to diabetes. Mom was still working at Shady Rest. She took on the added responsibility of caring for him. She was so worn out after coming home in the evenings that Dad made her quit the job at Shady Rest. The family no longer needed Mom's paycheck and Mom was content because she wasn't giving up nursing. Uncle Mike still needed her skills. Mom learned to drive at a local driving school so that the five daily trips she made to Uncle Mike's house would be easier. Mom spent at least six hours a day with Uncle Mike. She got him out of the bed at six in the morning, made his daily meals, made sure he took his medicine, helped him with toileting, bathed him, cleaned the house, did his laundry, and put him to bed in the evening. Mom barely had time to sleep. She kept up this demanding routine day after day until Uncle Mike died on September 12, 1985.

Stepa, my father's chauffeur from Germany, died December 13, 1973, after a car hit him while he crossed a street by their home in Chicago. Stepa's death was life-changing for my mother because of the events that followed. Stepa and Sofie owned a large apartment complex on 1055 E. 47th Street, several blocks west of the notorious Cabrini Green high-rises. They had purchased the apartment building in 1951 after they immigrated as displaced persons from Lübeck, Germany. At the time of the purchase, the neighborhood was transitioning from middle class to lower middle class. By the 1960s, it became part of the South Side ghetto. Cabrini Green was at the center of the most violent area of Chicago. I was at home from college at the time of Stepa's unfortunate death. Mom asked me to go to his funeral. Ines stayed home to take care of Uncle Mike. We were on standby in Denver for a flight to Midway Airport in Chicago. We all got on the flight but did not sit near one another. Mom ended up next to singer and actor Sammy Davis, Jr. He had just finished a show and was traveling with his bodyguards to Chicago. The show had worn him out and my mom sensed he was not wanting to chat with fans. But, after Sammy reluctantly began talking to Mom, he succumbed to her amazing personality. They spent the entire trip talking and laughing. We landed in a blizzard, but that didn't faze either of them. They continued their boisterous conversation while every other passenger on the plane was sick with fear. Sammy invited my mom to bring the entire family backstage to his performance that evening in Chicago. He was going to send a limo to pick us up and treat us to dinner. Mom told him we were in Chicago for the funeral of a family member, so we couldn't accept his kind offer. Sammy gave Mom his telephone number and said that she would always be welcome to visit.

We tried to catch a taxi to Sofie's apartment but had a hard time finding a driver who would make the trip into this dangerous neighborhood. Mom finally convinced a kind taxi driver who lived close to Sofie to take us. Once we arrived, the driver got out of the car and walked us right up to Sofie's door. He asked us to please be careful. Sofie answered the door with her two bulldogs barking behind her. The driver waited until we walked in and then left.

Mom and Dad spent the evening comforting Sofie. Only her friend Lulu, who lived on the second floor of the apartment complex, would visit after Stepa died. On our first night, a tenant knocked on the door around midnight. There was a plumbing issue with a bathroom faucet. Stepa had done his own janitorial work, and Sofie had no one to take over. I went upstairs and fixed the problem. I could see that Sofie couldn't handle the complex alone. So, I volunteered to stay after the funeral and help until the start of classes on January 10, 1974. It was a long month. The constant violence in the area made it hard to help Sofie. I could hear guns firing during the night. There were two break-in attempts during my stay, and a gang was lying in wait for me while I emptied the trash in the complex bin one night. I barely escaped. Sofie hired a person to take over the janitorial duties before I left. Then Ines flew to Chicago to be with Sofie for a month at the start of February.

Mom continued her breakneck schedule and ran two households. She volunteered at the church and worked in the soup kitchen. She and Dad kept up the farm. By the start of the 1970s, they no longer had livestock. If my father needed or wanted fresh meat, he purchased an animal from a farmer he knew, and they butchered and processed it before Dad brought the meat home. There was only one time that he had purchased livestock and did not butcher the animals at his friend's farm. He was planning on a celebration for his 60th birthday in 1973. He purchased seven young goats and transported them home. He asked our neighbor Lloyd to help him butcher the animals the next evening after work. He planned to roast them on a spit the next night for his birthday party. Dad tied them up in the barn and checked on them in the morning before he left for work. After Dad left, Mom was outside in the garden and heard the animals crying in the barn. They had tangled themselves up during the day, trying to work free. Mom felt sorry for the goats and tried to untangle them. She loosened their bindings, and they all wriggled free and jumped over the bottom half of the closed Dutch door entrance into the barn. Mom ran out to catch them, but the goats had all crawled under or jumped over the fences around our farm. The locals later confirmed that there were sightings of a new herd of wild goats around the Arkansas River bottom near our farm. Mom was so embarrassed. When Dad came home, he looked in the barn and saw only the ropes that the animals had slipped out of. He walked into the house stunned and asked Mom if she had seen or heard anything from the barn that day. Mom said no. My father went off muttering to himself.

In September 1974, Ines drove Mom to Fort Collins to visit me at Colorado State University on a sunny Saturday afternoon. She had not called before coming. Before lunch, one of my roommates had made a bet with the other roommate, and the loser had to streak around our apartment complex. When it came time to pay up, the loser stripped and then, with a rather large audience, began his streak around the complex. As he ran back to our apartment, he passed my mom and sister as they drove into the parking lot. They saw him run by the car and then up the stairs to my apartment door on the second floor. "Is that Butch's apartment?" Mom asked. Butch was her nickname for me when I was a young child. My sister said yes. "My God!" Mom responded. When Mom came up to the apartment, I had to explain what happened. My sister just laughed.

When Mom visited, word got around. My roommates and friends would show up like fruit flies, knowing that she brought a care package full of strudels, *potica,* baklava, cookies, and turnovers. Each one said hello and gave her a hug. She opened the pastry container and gave everyone a choice of delicacies. On the way back to Pueblo, she told me that she and Ines laughed. "So that is what Butch went to college for?" Mom said.

GRADUATE SCHOOL AND MARRIAGE

I graduated from Colorado State University with an engineering degree and started graduate school at the University of Illinois in June 1975. I then met my future wife, Rose, in October 1975 in the dining hall. During Christmas break, my friend Bob invited me to his house to attend a New Year's Eve party. I arrived on December 30 and stayed overnight. I called Rose, who lived 20 miles north in Elmhurst, on New Year's Eve morning to see if she wanted to go into Chicago with Bob and me. Rose was excited to hear from me and said she would meet me at Bob's house in Orland Park. Bob drove Rose and me to the Chicago Field Museum. We returned to Bob's house after spending the day in Chicago, and his parents invited Rose to stay for dinner. A major ice storm hit the Chicago area while we were eating. After seeing how bad the ice was, Rose called her mom, Genevieve, and asked if she could stay at Bob's house. Genevieve refused and told Rose to drive home anyway. When I went out to look at the ice, it was already a half-inch thick on the road. I would not let Rose drive home alone. I told Bob's mom that I was going to drive Rose home to Elmhurst. When she saw the ice, she put her foot down and said no. Bob's mom called Genevieve at the party she was attending and said there was no way she would let Rose leave in the ice storm. Rose's parents saw how bad the ice was and reluctantly agreed to let her stay. Bob's mom promised them she would chaperone. Rose was going to stay in the same room as Bob's sisters.

When Rose returned to the University of Illinois for the spring semester, we began dating seriously. During the summer break, I visited my parents in Colorado and they gave me the family car as a gift. I had to return in a couple of weeks and drove back to Urbana. I spent the fall semester of 1976 working on my research project and taking courses. I was preparing for an important experiment that would lead to a Ph.D., so I stayed in Illinois over the 1976 Christmas break.

My experiment worked the first time I tried it on February 22, 1977. My path to a Ph.D. had just become clear. I was so excited that I asked Rose to marry me. She said yes, and we shopped for an engagement ring together. I did not have the money to pay for it, but I put it on a six-month layaway and made monthly payments. We ended up visiting the ring every month when I brought in a payment.

In the spring of 1977, both sets of parents were concerned that Rose and I were getting too serious. We had not told them about purchasing a ring yet. They insisted on meeting each other. I was naïve enough to set the meeting at the only place I knew in Chicago, Sofie's home. Rose's parents almost did not show up because they were afraid of the neighborhood. I met them in front of Sofie's apartment complex and led them inside. Fortunately, Mom's best friend, Ynes, now lived on the North Side of Chicago in a safe neighborhood. After leaving Lübeck, Ynes had wandered throughout Germany until she met her future husband. Then they immigrated to the United States in 1955 and settled in Chicago. Mom had kept in touch with her over the years. Mom called Ynes and she insisted we come to her home. Everyone was glad to get out of Sofie's place. We drove to Ynes's home, which was near the house where Rose's father had grown up. Ynes and her family prepared a nice dinner for us and we spent a lovely evening together.

I ended up paying off the ring in August 1977. Rose was excited, but she said that she could not wear it until I asked her father for permission. She invited me to her house for a weekend. It was during the visit that I asked Rose's father for permission to marry her. He forcefully said no. Rose was heartbroken, but we both agreed that it would not stop us. I called my parents and told them I was getting engaged. They were unhappy as well.

I had not made a good impression with Rose's parents either time we met. They continued to object to our engagement. They threatened to disown Rose. In fear of losing financial support from her parents, she found a job at the University of Illinois computer center in the fall of 1977 to pay for college. She worked there for a year. Then Rose found a higher-paying job at the state water survey, where she worked until she graduated in 1979.

Sofie eventually decided she could not keep up with the apartment complex, so when a buyer made an offer, she accepted and closed in the fall of 1977. Sofie moved to Pueblo because Mom and Dad were her only friends. She lived with my parents initially. Mom cooked and cleaned for her. Sofie was grossly obese and did not walk well. She had a light complexion, with red hair, a large bulb-shaped nose, and was very introverted. She had a multitude of health issues that required Mom's nursing skills. After a year, Sofie hired a contractor to build a house in a development near Sunset Park. It took another 11 months before she could move in. Sofie's house was about ten blocks from my uncle's place, so Mom made stops at both Sofie's house and Uncle Mike's house three times a day to provide care. Sofie and Mike were jealous of each other because they had to share Mom's attention. They each became more childlike and demanding. My sister told me horror stories about Mom's problems. But it didn't stop Mom. She had survived a war and knew how to handle conflicts.

To make matters worse, Dad retired in 1978. He had worked all his life and did not take retirement well. We all thought that Dad would live a long time because of the longevity of his family. His mother, father, and siblings who had survived the war all lived well into their 80s. My sister and I thought that Mom was the sickly parent and that Dad would outlive her. But Dad drank heavily after he retired. He was also very demanding of my mom's time. His retirement meant that she had to manage three adults who had, in effect, descended into their second childhoods.

Rose and I made it official before Christmas of 1978 that we planned to get married after graduation in May 1979. Rose's parents still did not like me and were not happy. When they realized that we were going to wed regardless of their opposition, Genevieve took over the planning. She picked out the date and decided that we would have a traditional Catholic ceremony. Genevieve made reservations at their parish church for the nuptials and chose the venue for the reception. The priest from the parish gave us a questionnaire to fill out. The questions were strange. We had to attest to so many things we did not believe, like agreeing to raise our children Catholic, that we eloped. A judge married us at the Urbana, Illinois, courthouse on May 21, 1979. That only caused more friction between Rose and her parents and gave them more reasons to hate me. My parents did not like the idea of me marrying Rose either. But I told them in no uncertain terms that if they wanted to be part of my life, they had to accept it. My parents were not happy, but they bit their tongues and swallowed their pride. Ultimately, they accepted our marriage.

Despite their opposition to our union, both of our families wanted to host separate receptions for us. Rose and I agreed. We first went to Chicago in mid-June for a reception at a dinner theater attended by Rose's immediate family. We had an excellent dinner and watched the floor show. Thankfully, the night ended quickly.

In July, we went to my parents' home. There were many rows of picnic tables and pits with goat and pig roasting on spits. My mom had baked every pastry in her repertoire and a wedding cake. There were several 16-gallon kegs of beer in ice baths around the tables and gallons of my dad's homemade wines. It seemed like every person I had met during my life had shown up for the reception. Rose and I had hoped to avoid a large reception, but this was typical of a party that my parents would throw. We both gritted our teeth and let my parents enjoy the moment.

DAD'S DEATH

I took a job as an assistant professor at a major midwestern university and started in August 1979. My academic career went very well. In 1984, I was in the first group of young academics to receive the Presidential Young Investigator Award. The Reagan Administration started the program to encourage the brightest scholars to pursue careers in academia. My mom and dad shared the newspaper clippings from the award with all their friends and acquaintances. They were extremely proud.

In 1982, my sister, Ines, had to find a new career. At 38, she started college at the University of Southern Colorado. She worked in the financial aid office while taking coursework. She majored in computer science and automotive engineering.

Things were not going smoothly with Mom. She continued to care for Sofie and Uncle Mike, but also found that my father needed a lot of attention after retirement. Caregiving was not a safe calling. In the summer of 1985, Mom fell at Uncle Mike's house and suffered broken ribs along with a concussion.

Dad's drinking caused his health to decline quickly. A catalyzing event that led him to drink even more was the death of Uncle Mike from a heart attack on September 12, 1985. Mike was Dad's only living sibling. I could not come to the funeral because Rose was seven months pregnant and was having complications.

My daughter, Natalia, was born by C-section on November 13, 1985. With Rose recovering, I needed to care for Natalia. Mom could not help us out because of her obligations in Colorado. Rose's mom and dad were still being disagreeable, so we could not count on them.

The next year was tumultuous. Both sides of the family were pressuring us to have Natalia baptized. Rose had also grown up in the Roman Catholic Church, but both of us had horrible experiences in Catholic school. We did not want our children to be raised Roman Catholic. We were determined that our daughter would have women role models in leadership positions. After doing research, we converted to a Protestant denomination that allowed women to be ministers and bishops. Natalia was baptized when she was nine months old. Mom and Dad understood our decision. Mom believed that there were many paths to finding God. She was simply happy for us. Rose's parents already had grandchildren who had been baptized in a Protestant denomination and said little.

Uncle Mike had left his house to Mom in appreciation for taking care of him. Mom did not know what to do with the house. She went back and forth on the idea of selling it, but my parents' friend Steve, who was a landlord, convinced her to rent the house. So, her venture into being a landlord began. She had two renters over the next two years, and they were nothing but trouble. The first set of renters was a couple who broke every appliance at least once during the year they were in the house. Mom spent more money fixing things and repairing damage than she collected from rent. Then there was a young couple who had three children. They looked nice and had references, but they wrecked the house even more than the first set of renters. About halfway through their lease, the couple moved out without telling Mom. They had destroyed the sewer line. Mom found out from the plumber that the damage was caused by the wife's art business. She made plaster sculptures in the basement and flushed the excess plaster down the toilet. There was a hardened plaster blockage in the sewer line that the plumber could not remove. The only way to repair it was to replace the line, which cost $10,000. She had to sell Uncle Mike's house in 1987 to cover the cost of the repair.

In February 1986, Dad was hospitalized with congestive heart failure. The doctors did not think he would survive. Mom asked if we could bring Natalia to Colorado so that Dad could see his grandchild before he died. We were worried about traveling with a three-month-old but wanted Dad to see his granddaughter. So, we made the trip by plane. Since Natalia was so young, Rose and I were concerned about exposing her to viruses and bacteria. We set the ground rules over the phone with Mom before we came. Only she would be allowed to hold Natalia. When Sofie demanded to hold her, I refused. Sofie was furious with me and there was a rift between us that never healed. When we brought Natalia into Dad's hospital room, he perked up. He touched her hand. That night, his heart arrhythmia stabilized and his prognosis improved. The doctors believed that seeing his granddaughter was responsible for his improvement. They released Dad from the hospital a few days later. We stayed a couple more days so he could be with Natalia and then I needed to return to the university to teach.

Mom's life got much harder after Dad came home. Mom fell again and broke her ribs and suffered another concussion while caring for Sofie in 1986. Watching Dad was a full-time job by itself. He continued to drink heavily. Dad bought whiskey and hid the bottles. Mom and Ines found most of the bottles and poured them down the sink. But they could not find all the alcohol. Sofie also became more demanding of her time. I don't know how Mom managed.

In 1987, the Department of Energy recruited me for an exchange program where I served as a senior scientist on a defense project for a year at Idaho National Laboratory. It was a tough year for everyone. Rose was pregnant with our son, Alex. The stress on Mom caring for two demanding people continued until Sofie's death on November 11, 1987. I could not attend Sofie's funeral because Rose needed help at home.

Soon after, we returned to the university from Idaho, in December 1987. Alex was born on April 19, 1988. He had the same official date of birth as my father. Dad's health declined rapidly during 1988, and he was again admitted to the hospital on December 4, 1988. His spleen was failing. He desperately wanted to see his grandson because he knew he didn't have long to live. I traveled to Colorado with Alex by plane. The doctor agreed to release Dad from the hospital for the afternoon so he could be with Alex. He couldn't do much because his illness had taken so much of his strength. He had to be carried into the house. Dad sat in his favorite chair with his grandson in his lap and talked to him. When we took Dad back to the hospital, everyone could tell there was no hope he would leave the hospital. I made it home with Alex on December 8. Mom called on December 11 to tell me that Dad had passed away. She was by his side. They had reminisced about their life in Europe during his last hours. The last thing he said was that he was sorry about all the pain that he caused her and that she was a wonderful woman. I went back to Pueblo for the funeral while Rose stayed home with Natalia and Alex.

Ines had a hard time with Dad's illness and death. Despite their checkered history, they had a close bond. She had never married. Ines took a lot of time off her job in the financial aid office at the university, and when her vacation and sick leave ran out, she took unpaid leave. The office manager was getting impatient with Ines and put her under additional stress. When Dad died, Ines became depressed. Her last semester at the University of Southern Colorado was a struggle. But she fought through her depression, did well in her classes, and graduated in May 1989. Afterward, Ines moved to Chicago, where she began working for Raytheon as a subcontractor to the Federal Aviation Administration. She handled the blueprints for the control towers and control systems at airports throughout the United States. She did very well at Raytheon. She won an award from the FAA in recognition for her work with the airports in the Great Lakes region. After they sold her division to Parson, she won another award for outstanding service.

RETURN TO EUROPE

Mom was lost after Dad's death. She continued volunteering at the church's soup kitchen, but it was only a temporary respite from her grief. She did not want to see her friends. Mom spent long periods of time alone sitting on the couch, lost in thought. Ines and I worried about her. Rose proposed that I take her to Europe. I had a scientific conference in Venice, Italy, at the end of March 1989, and I asked her to come along. The pretext was that I wanted her to show me Lübeck, where she had been a slave laborer and then a displaced person. I also wanted to meet her family in Yugoslavia. The stop in Venice, a city which she dearly loved and had not seen since 1935, would be the icing on the cake. It hardly took any convincing because it was important to Mom that I meet the people and see the places that were integral to her life. Mom was a candidate for knee replacement by then, and I had some concern about her ability to walk. But Europe turned out to be therapeutic. It was as if the clock had turned back 20 years. We walked everywhere, and she never complained about her knees hurting.

Once in Lübeck, Mom wanted to see if her friend Hilda was still alive and to visit my dad's cousin, Father Kordiš, who was in a retirement home for priests in Lübeck. We found Hilda in the phone book. Mom called Hilda and told her who we were. Hilda cried with joy and begged us to come over for lunch. When Hilda gave us her address, Mom recognized it as being close to the hotel where she and Dad once lived. We spent the afternoon and evening with Hilda. She and Mom reminisced and then talked about their lives after Mom and Dad had immigrated. We stayed a long time and finally had to leave. Hilda and Mom exchanged contact information and phone numbers. They kept in touch until Hilda's death in 2009.

The next day, we visited Father Kordiš. He was suffering from the onset of Alzheimer's. We met outside of the retirement home and sat on a park bench on a beautiful, sunny day, which was rare for that month in northern Germany. Father Kordiš wanted to know about my father. When he learned that Dad had died a few months back, you could see his spirit dim. When Mom introduced me as Jure's son to Father Kordiš, he told me, "Your father was a great man." Mom talked at great length about our life in the U.S. When an evening breeze stirred in the air, Father Kordiš said that he needed to leave so he would not miss supper. We walked him to the door of the retirement center. Mom hugged Father Kordiš and he gave both of us a blessing. We caught a bus back to the hotel and had supper at a restaurant nearby. Mom saw that they had poached flounder on the menu and then talked to the server about its preparation. She looked at me and said, "I dislike fish, but the way they prepare this dish is special." We both ordered it and Mom was right; it was special. It tasted like butter. That was the only time I ever saw Mom eat fish. I asked her why she chose the flounder and she responded that the dish brought back a cherished memory of my father.

We dedicated the next day to one of the main reasons that Mom wanted to return to Lübeck. Mom had read an article about slave laborers forced to work for German companies during the war. The German government had just approved a pension for slave laborers who had worked in Germany. She gathered up proof of her confinement as a slave laborer amongst the papers she had carefully saved when she had immigrated to the U.S. The amount of money involved was minuscule, but it was a matter of pride and a symbol to have the German government pay her for the suffering that she had endured. There was a determination in her eyes that I could not dissuade. The government office in Lübeck would not accept her papers and claimed that an Allied air raid during the war had destroyed the official records. Her application for a pension was denied. This simply rubbed salt in the wound. She was upset for days. I later heard that the German government had done the same thing to others who made claims. The whole gesture had been for show, not a true reckoning.

Mom's last goal in Lübeck was to look Dimitri in the eye. He was my father's closest and most trusted friend, and he had betrayed Dad. It was Dimitri who had swindled my father before he immigrated. Dimitri had purchased my dad's factory and its inventory on credit because my dad was so desperate to leave Germany. Dimitri then refused to pay Dad. He was also the person who hid from my mom when she needed help after being released from quarantine. Looking Dimitri in the eye after 36 years was not as satisfying as my mom had thought it would be. He was a broken man living in a dilapidated warehouse. His diabetes was clearly out of control. Dimitri's right leg had been amputated as a result.

The next day, Mom wanted to go to the beach where she used to swim. No one was there because the water was too cold, and the weather was not warm. But I could imagine her in her prime, swimming on this beach. When I looked at her, she was deep in thought, probably remembering a time when she was young. We left the next day. By then we had spent five days in Lübeck.

Then we traveled to Venice to attend my scientific conference. Mom enjoyed seeing Venice again. Her last visit had been in 1935, when she went there on vacation with her mother, Inga, and Yelca. Mom wandered the streets and shopped while I attended the meeting. When I skipped some sessions, Mom showed me sights that she had visited as a young girl. On the last night of the conference, we attended a banquet. It was an exquisite, themed affair, replicating a feast from 1750 Venice. We arrived at the banquet hall in gondolas.

Staff dressed in 18th-century servant costumes greeted us. The halls were lit by candlelight. On the ground floor of the building, period-appropriate hors d'oeuvres were served with wine. Mom and I sampled them all.

It was the first time that I had tried Beluga caviar. A Russian scientist named Andre, who demonstrated the fine points of enjoying Beluga caviar, befriended us. My mom had been a hit with countless people at the social. She talked with so many that I could not keep track. The servants then invited us upstairs to the banquet hall, where Mom and I sat at an empty round table. Once we sat down, the many acquaintances she had made during the social hour scrambled to grab seats at our table. It filled up quickly and those who could not sit with Mom sat at the tables surrounding us. It was an elegant banquet, and Mom was the center of attention. After the banquet, we had to pack our bags because we needed to catch an early-morning train to Zagreb.

POPOVAČA

In Zagreb, Mom learned what had been a closely guarded family secret. Her oldest brother, Alojz, was still alive. We met with Alojz, his wife, his daughter Branka, and grandson in the basement of their house. They asked that we not mention anything about Alojz since they were afraid if the communist regime knew he was alive, they would arrest him. Alojz had been a member of the partisans during the war. In late 1943, he had had his fill of fighting and deserted to be with his one true love. Everyone believed that the partisans had executed Alojz. However, it was all a ruse. He had hidden in the basement of his wife's home. Alojz did not leave the basement until the communist government of Yugoslavia crumbled and Croatia declared independence on June 25, 1991. He was 79 years old when he was finally free. Mom was so happy that Alojz was alive. She was also excited to meet Branka and her son, who sang Mom a Croatian folk song. They had extraordinary voices. Both were members of a Croatian singing group. When we left, Mom and Alojz hugged. He told Mom that we could contact him through his oldest daughter, Danica.

We stayed with Danica and her husband, Ivan. Jasmin, Danica's daughter, and her husband, also named Ivan, visited with us as well.

Mom had an extraordinary time with Danica and Ivan. Ivan loved to tell jokes, and he made Mom laugh so hard that tears streamed down her cheeks.

Mom wanted to visit Pepic, and Danica arranged for us to travel to Popovača to see him and his family. They lived in the farmhouse that Grandfather built. Mom finally forgave her younger brother. Up to that point, she had had no communication with him since Yelca's death in 1947. Mom was angry about his treatment of Yelca while she was dying from Lou Gehrig's Disease. When we met Pepic, Mom said that she was disappointed with him for not treating Yelca well. Pepic apologized and said that he had never forgiven himself.

We stayed with Pepic and his wife for two days. I was able to see the house that grandfather had built and the farm where Mom grew up. Stories about her childhood came to life for me. I saw the pond where she had learned how to swim and the schoolhouse where she had gotten into trouble. I could picture her sitting at the kitchen table as a young, strong-willed little girl with big dreams.

We visited my grandfather's and grandmother's graves, and Mom was saddened to see that old wooden crosses were used as markers. She asked Pepic why they didn't have gravestones. Pepic said that they could not afford anything more. Mom desperately wanted to talk to a stone carver but could not get an appointment in time.

There were some other things Mom wanted to accomplish in the short time we had left. She asked Pepic about her half-sister Marie, and the teacher, Miss Marta, who had hit her. It turned out that both were still living in Popovača. Mom requested to see them. Pepic arranged for Mom to see Marta. When we arrived, Mom looked Marta squarely in the eye. "Do you remember the little girl who you hit?"

Marta smiled. "Yes, but I did not hit you very hard, Katicà." Mom laughed and introduced me. She said that I was a university professor in the United States. They hugged when we departed. Pepic said that he had contacted Marie, but she did not want to see Mom, which broke Mom's heart.

Mom made one more request. She wanted to visit her youngest sister, Dragica. Pepic warned us that Dragica lived in squalor. She had been married to an abusive husband who beat her severely. One outcome of the beatings was a fractured skull that had not healed right, so her head was misshapen, and she was partially deaf. Dragica had a 17-year-old daughter living with her who was an unwed mother. When we went to Dragica's home, it was as bad as we were told. As soon as I walked in, hungry fleas jumped on my arm and bit me. Dragica hugged Mom and then me. You could see that she had suffered a great deal during her life. Her daughter had young-looking eyes, but she seemed old, and her teeth were rotten. I had seen methamphetamine users in the States, and she had all the signs of being addicted. The baby was adorable. I felt sorry for her starting life in this way. I gave Dragica a considerable sum of money, which I requested be used for the care of her granddaughter. I figured there was enough to change the baby's life. I only hoped that it would go to the baby and not drugs. Mom left Dragica with cash as well.

Before we left Popovača, Mom asked Pepic to have gravestones made for their parents. She asked him how much it would cost, and he estimated $1,000, which she gave him in cash and made him promise to use it to purchase the gravestones. Mom learned a year later from Danica that Pepic had kept the money. Mom was resolved to make another trip to Popovača to talk to a stone carver herself and get the marker put on the graves of her parents.

Even though she did not achieve all that she wanted, our trip was still a success. After visiting her surviving relatives in Zagreb and the small town of Popovača where she grew up on my grandfather's farm, she finally turned the corner from her grief. She seemed like her old self. Mom wanted to be with people again. Her life centered on volunteer work at the church and spending time with friends. She loved to invite the widows and widowers from her and Dad's old social circle over for a home-cooked meal. It was comforting to Ines and me since we could not be near her. Mom's friends watched over her. Her life was active, vibrant, and had purpose again.

There were nagging problems that Mom now had the strength to confront. She could no longer keep up with the farm. She made the hard choice to sell it. Fortunately, the farm sold quickly to a family friend. I met Ines in Pueblo to help Mom pack and move. My parents had accumulated a lifetime of possessions. We held a garage sale and sold what we could. Mom gave many of the items to charity and friends. The rest we moved into a new house. It was a grueling two-week job.

Over the next five years, Rose's and my children, Natalia and Alex, were old enough that we could drive from our home in the Midwest to Colorado for summer vacations. Grandma Katheryn was more than happy to spoil them, and they adored her. We had a minivan and took Mom on day trips into the mountains. Mom loved driving in the cool mountain air. It was a nice getaway from the summer heat of the high plains. Her favorite places were San Isabel, where the kids loved to explore Bishop's Castle, and Cascade, Colorado, where the kids enjoyed Santa's Workshop. She was a wonderful grandmother who showered the kids with love at every opportunity. It was fortunate that they had her, because Rose's parents did not treat them well.

DECLINING HEALTH

Mom had a series of health issues when she was almost 70. First, she was diagnosed with congestive heart failure. The doctor put her on a strict diet and gave her a blood thinner called Warfarin. On this medication, she no longer could eat vegetables with green leaves. Some of the foods that she loved the most, like lettuce, were now off limits because they had too much vitamin K, which counteracted the blood thinning properties of Warfarin.

Then she was diagnosed with breast cancer in April 1992. She had a mastectomy within a week of the diagnosis. Aunt Inga traveled to Colorado and stayed with her for a month. About a year after her mastectomy, her doctor discovered that she had Type 2 diabetes. They put her on Metformin and a low-carb diet, which kept her away from some of her other favorite foods, such as bread and butter. But Mom had great discipline. She avoided foods rich in vitamin K and carbohydrates. She was able to control her blood sugar through diet and Metformin alone.

I did not see her in 1992 because I had accepted a Fulbright Fellowship to the University of New South Wales in Australia. It was difficult being away from the States. I could not help with any of Mom's health problems. Our kids were young, and it was a challenge just getting to Australia. My time in Australia was rich with some of our most cherished moments together as a family.

When we returned from Australia, I visited Mom in the summer of 1993 with Alex and Natalia. Mom was not herself. She could barely walk and had lost her energy. Nonetheless, in August, despite poor health and failing knees, she made a return trip to Europe with Ines. They visited Lübeck and Croatia. Ines rented a car in Germany to spare Mom the effort of walking. Mom made sure that Ines visited the camp where she had been held as a slave laborer, the remains of the underground Volkswagen factory where she worked, and the apartment where Ines grew up. They also went to see one place that Mom loved while she lived in Lübeck, the beach at Strandkorb Travemunde. Mom always swam in the Baltic Sea near Lübeck, and before that, when she lived in Croatia, she swam in the Adriatic Sea. Mom told Ines that one thing she missed about Europe was the sea. The only place that she could swim when she first came to Pueblo was at the YWCA pool, and it was like a bathtub compared to what she was used to.

The trip to Croatia was risky because Serbia and Croatia were still at war over Croatia's declaration of independence. Luckily, the fighting had moved south and there was no activity near Zagreb. They could get into Zagreb by train and then Ines rented a car to drive Mom around the area. They visited relatives in Zagreb and Popovača. Mom's primary purpose for that trip was to make sure that the wooden crosses on her parents' graves were replaced with headstones. It was more complicated to get done than she had thought. The stone carver did not accept American dollars. He would take only German marks. Mom and Ines had to find a bank in Zagreb willing to cash traveler's checks for marks. They drove for hours before they found a bank that could make the transaction. They exchanged 1,000 American dollars for German marks. The cash filled a paper bag. They drove back to Popovača and the stone carver accepted the bag of cash. He carved the grave markers as promised. Since Mom no longer trusted Pepic, she asked Danica to take pictures of the gravestones. When she finally saw the pictures that her niece had taken, Mom was ecstatic. I think she felt guilty that she had not seen her parents since the Nazis took her from their farm in 1941. It was one of her goals in life to honor them. That goal had finally been achieved.

Mom had her knees replaced in August 1994. She scheduled both knees on the same day, despite the surgeon's objection to a double knee replacement. He had recommended doing one at a time. Mom's said she would not wait another day to get both knees fixed. The doctor learned the hard way that Mom never took no for an answer. I was involved in a project keeping Russian scientists from selling know-how about the production of weapons of mass destruction to rogue nations. My schedule involved constant travel to and from the former Soviet Union. I was unsuccessful in trying to convince my mom to wait until I was back in the States. Ines went to Pueblo for Mom's surgery, but she had to leave shortly afterward. Mom went through the therapy alone. Two weeks later, when Ines could get time off to return, Mom was already walking with a cane. The therapist told Ines that she had never seen a patient recover from double knee replacement that fast. Nothing about Mom's ability to overcome the worst possible circumstances surprised me. Her life was about achieving the impossible.

Mom was excited about rehab because it included water therapy. She was in the pool for hours every day. Mom told Ines that if she had known how easy it was to have double knee surgery, she would have done it years earlier. The positive that came out of this risky surgery was her knees did not hurt anymore. But the doctor had put Mom on oxygen at night. So, now she had an oxygen concentrator and a hospital bed in the house. Mom never told us why she needed them. It worried both Ines and me. Mom refused to move either to Chicago or to my home. She stubbornly wanted to stay in her own house. There was no way to win this argument, so I got her a First Alert device.

The artificial knee joints allowed Mom to do the things she loved most. She continued volunteering at the church where she cooked in the soup kitchen. Mom was active in various clubs. In the Croatian Club, she taught children and adults Croatian. In another, she became involved in Tamburica, a Croatian folk music and dance group. Mom taught the members about the meanings and traditions behind the music, songs, and dances. She socialized with old friends and made new friends.

The head of the language department at the University of Southern Colorado heard about my mom's expertise in teaching Croatian at the club. She wanted to increase the course offerings in her department and asked Mom to teach first- and second-year courses in Croatian. Mom agreed to become an instructor and taught night classes. Her courses were extremely popular; she filled the seats. Mom had to give up teaching in the fall of 1997 because it required too much of her time. However, she continued going to the pool for workouts with friends. Her mind was sharp, and she had regained some of her boundless energy. It seemed that age would never catch up with her. But that was wishful thinking.

In 1998, Natalia and I visited Mom during the summer, and we noticed a change. While we were there, four or five people a day would drop in to see her. After each visit, Mom would confess that she was tired of all the visitors. This was not like her; company had always brightened her spirits. One day, Mom saw a friend and her two children park in front of the house. Mom locked the front door and looked at Natalia and me and said, "Don't answer the door." The friend was persistent in trying to open the door. Then she and her children started looking through the windows in the house. Mom told Natalia and me to follow her into the basement. Then her friend and children began looking through the basement windows. Mom instructed us to join her while she hid in a storage closet under the stairs. Natalia refused and simply went into a downstairs bedroom. Natalia was taken by surprise when one of the kids investigated the bedroom window. Eventually, Mom's friend and her children went to Mom's backyard. There was an entrance to the garage where the prior owner had installed a dog door. The youngest child crawled through the dog door and we heard him open the garage. As Mom and I huddled in the storage closet, she looked at me in horror and said, "The door between the house and the garage is open." At that moment, her friend and the children entered the house, yelling my mom's name at the top of their lungs. They began a systematic search of the rooms upstairs. Then they came downstairs and found Natalia in the bedroom. They asked Natalia where Katheryn was. She responded, "I am her granddaughter. What are you doing in her house? You woke me up." Then Natalia said, "I have no idea where my grandmother is." The friend and her children began opening the doors to all the rooms downstairs. Finally, the youngest child opened the door to the closet where we were hiding. "Here they are, Mom!" he yelled. I was embarrassed. We sheepishly walked upstairs with her and the children. No explanations were made or demanded. Her friend stayed and talked nonstop for four hours before she finally left. We couldn't get a word in. Afterward, Mom looked at me and said, "That is why I hid."

In 1999, I went to Washington, D.C., to serve in the U.S. Department of State as a William C. Foster Fellow. I worked in the Bureau of Arms Control and provided expertise on Russian nuclear weapons for the START 3 negotiations. Unfortunately, START 3 was dead soon after I arrived. I was then asked to provide expertise on the risk of technology transfer between impoverished Soviet scientists and bad actors around the world.

I continually worried about Mom's increasing desire to be left alone. This was not like her. But there was little I could do since I was so far away from Pueblo. All I could do was call her daily.

Mom had many more incidents of not wanting to answer the door when friends visited. It got to be a game between her and the close friends who monitored her. On her 80th birthday in 2002, Mom had learned through trial and error to lock all the doors into the house and fasten the chain lock on the front door. One of the friends who monitored her, Anna, had a key. Anna brought over a group of people and a cake to celebrate Mom's birthday. This time Mom hid in the upstairs clothes closet behind some dresses. Anna used her key to open the bolt but found that the door was still chain-locked. Her husband used his pocket knife to work the chain lock out of its holder through the narrow opening. They were able to get in. The group then searched for my mom and eventually found her behind the dresses in the clothes closet. Mom's only comment was, "What good is a chain lock?"

I believe that Mom became more introverted because many of her close friends had recently died. She lost the desire to be with people for fear that one of them would soon pass away. She would be inconsolable for weeks after a friend's death. Mom once confided to me after the passing of a close friend ten years her junior, "I wish that God would take me."

One of the most distressing days in Mom's life occurred when Anna had a stroke in 2004 and passed away two days later. Anna could not talk, but Mom held her hand and reminisced. Mom could tell by looking into her eyes that Anna knew she did not have long to live. Mom was with her when she died. This had a profound impact on her. She became a recluse after that, although she still went to the soup kitchen to serve food. But there were only a few people whom she wanted to see. One was Uncle Phillip's grandson, Martin. He was her godson, and they were close. Another was Steve, who always helped her by fixing things that broke around the house. He was a widower and loved to come over every Sunday after church for freshly baked strudel and coffee. Nonetheless, I worried about her, so I once again asked her to move in with us. Ines wanted her to move to Chicago. She refused both of us. Pueblo was her home, and she intended to stay put.

About the only good thing that happened to her in 2004 was that Natalia graduated from high school and began her freshman year at North Central College in the fall. Her granddaughter was going to college, and it made her so proud.

THE FALL

Ines and I worried about Mom, so we constantly reached out to her. Ines phoned her once or twice a day. I called three or four times a week. Mom seemed to be doing well. Then on May 30, 2005, after I returned from a trip to India where I worked on setting up exchange agreements with some universities, I talked to Mom and something was off. I couldn't put my finger on it. So, I called Ines and asked her if she noticed anything wrong. My sister became concerned and called Mom. She also got the sense that something wasn't right. Ines then asked our cousin Martin to check in on Mom. When Martin got to the house, Mom did not answer the door, so he looked through the picture window and saw her on the floor. She had fallen about eight hours earlier and could not get up. Her leg had swollen with blood from internal bleeding caused by her blood thinner. Mom had the cordless phone and a First Alert around her neck, but she had been too stubborn to summon help. Martin called 911. Mom was taken to the emergency room. The doctor told Martin that she could not have lasted much longer without medical attention. During treatment in the emergency room, Mom's heart stopped. While she was being resuscitated, Mom believed that she had seen Heaven. She was on top of a hill, thick with green grass, and below there was a beautiful meadow. There she saw my father with her parents, her grandparents, Mike, Mary, Sofie, Stepa, and other friends and relatives. They were waving and beckoning her to come down. She tried to walk toward them, but something stopped her. Then she woke up.

When Ines found out about Mom's heart stopping, she immediately took emergency leave and caught a flight to Colorado Springs. I made it to Pueblo a day later. After two days, Mom was progressing well, and we thought that the doctors would release her soon. But they ordered an MRI before they would let her leave. I had gone out for some lunch and when I got back, Mom's primary care physician was having a serious conversation with my sister. The MRI technician had erroneously injected Mom with the contrast agent gadolinium. When I heard the news, it upset me. I knew that you don't give a patient with congestive heart failure gadolinium because of the medications patients take to excrete fluids from the kidneys. Gadolinium causes nephrogenic systemic fibrosis in people with weakened kidneys. Mom's kidneys had ceased to function.

The hospital's chief of staff took over my mom's care from that point on. They hoped that her kidney function would return and that she could expel the gadolinium from her system. I caught a flight back home. I wanted to bring Alex to Pueblo so he could see his grandmother. I did not think Mom would survive long. It took about two and a half weeks for her kidneys to regain 40 percent of their prior function. But she ended up staying in the hospital for three additional months until they could stabilize her. If they had not mistakenly given her gadolinium, she would have gone home the day after her MRI.

By the end of her hospital stay, Mom was weak, and the doctors did not think that she would walk again. They released her to a nursing home for therapy. Mom had worked in a nursing home and knew that most of the staff paid little attention to the patients. She begged to go home, but the doctors were adamant that she needed to be in a step-down facility. I had to return to the university since I was scheduled to give a speech at a conference that I was co-chairing. Ines stayed with Mom at the nursing home. It was as bad as Mom had feared; the staff ignored calls for help. Ines refused to leave Mom alone, so she slept in her room. Under the stressful conditions of a nursing home, Mom experienced some chest pains and went to the hospital emergency room. The doctors determined that the chest pain was from anxiety. They wanted to send her back to the nursing home, but Ines put her foot down and demanded that they release Mom into her care. Mom's primary care doctor told Ines that Mom would never walk again and needed to stay in a nursing home for the rest of her life. But Ines reminded the doctor and the hospital about the gadolinium mishap. She got the doctor to release Mom into her care. He reluctantly ordered visiting therapists to work with Mom at home and a visiting nurse to come in and take vitals three times a day. Once home, Mom gained strength and could eventually walk. She decided to change her physician a few weeks later. Mom made a special trip to her old doctor's office once she could walk again to show him how well she was doing. He was not happy to see her.

Ines had used up all her leave, and the company demanded that she return to work or she would be laid off. Ines would not abandon Mom again. She allowed the company to lay her off so she could receive unemployment insurance. She was two years away from being able to collect social security and five years from being on Medicare. The company had to hire four people to do her job and, even then, they could not keep up with the work. They tried to hire Ines back, but she was resolute to stay in Pueblo and care for Mom.

Five months after Mom was released from the hospital, Ines saw an ad on television from a law firm that was litigating the use of gadolinium contrast agents and adverse reactions. She called the number. My mother had lost about 60 percent of her kidney function because of gadolinium. The law firm wanted Mom's medical records, so Ines started the arduous task of getting copies of the records from the hospital. When the records arrived, she found that the hospital had taken out all references to Mom's MRI. The law firm was not interested in the case unless Ines could provide them with documentation that showed Mom had had an MRI with a gadolinium contrast agent.

Ines had stayed with Mom day and night at the hospital and attended every test. She had been with Mom when they performed the MRI. So, she knew that the hospital had done something fishy with the records and talked with me. I called Mom's old primary care physician to obtain a copy of the files, since he had ordered the MRI and had disclosed the use of gadolinium to Ines and me. He refused to provide any records or write a letter that would contradict the hospital. The doctor was afraid of losing his hospital privileges. Ines then obtained a copy of the hospital's billing records. They showed that Medicare had been billed for not one but three MRIs. We now had the evidence that the hospital was paid for the one MRI where they used a gadolinium contrast agent. Plus, we found out that they had overcharged Medicare for two additional MRIs that Mom never had. So, Ines confronted the hospital about the discrepancy between the records and billing. The hospital lawyered up and refused to speak with us. We searched nationally for another attorney to take the case on contingency, but nobody was interested. We could not afford the out-of-pocket expenses to pay for an extended lawsuit, so we gave up. Ines, however, reported the hospital's fraudulent billing to the Inspector General.

THE TRAGEDY

In 2006, Alex graduated from high school and began attending the university where I worked. This cheered up Mom considerably. Both of her grandchildren were now in college. Mom continued to improve. The major reason was Ines. Mom remained active with the soup kitchen, teaching at Croatian Club and Tamburica. It looked like she finally shed the trouble that always seemed to follow her during life.

Then, on December 11, 2007, disaster struck our family. My son Alex was driving to the university to take his last final exam of the fall semester in his sophomore year. He was in an accident and his heart had stopped. An off-duty firefighter was passing by and saw Alex's lifeless body. He checked for a pulse. When he couldn't find one, he started CPR and called for an ambulance. Even though the hospital was only a half-mile away, the ambulance arrived 15 minutes later. They took Alex to the ER, and it required three shocks with a paddle to restart his heart. They estimated that about 25 minutes had passed before Alex's heart was restarted. He suffered an anoxic brain injury.

I called Ines and told her what had happened, but I made her promise to keep it from Mom. It worried me that this tragedy on the anniversary of my father's death would affect Mom's health. But she knew something was wrong. She had had a dream about Alex's accident the night before it occurred. Mom would not stop asking questions about Alex, so we had to tell her. Alex was in a coma for 21 days. The doctors gave us a spectrum of opinions that ranged from "He will never wake up" to "He is young so he still can pull out of the coma." Mom insisted that Alex would wake up and prayed for him constantly. Rose and I took turns sitting with him in the ICU. We did research on patients in a coma and learned that music and familiar smells were helpful. We brought in Alex's classic rock CD collection and continually cycled through the music. His favorite group was Jethro Tull, so we played their albums more frequently. He loved the smell of pumpkin pie, so we brought in pumpkin pie spice as well as other spices and aromas. Alex loved comedy, so we also turned on the comedy channel. I knew long before the doctors and nurses that my son was waking up. He responded appropriately during comedy routines. The nurses and doctors were never around for the good parts of the routines, so when I called them in, inevitably the comedy was not so good, and he did not respond. One day a nurse was in the room when something funny was on and Alex responded. She watched him closely, and he kept responding to the humorous parts of the routine. She called in the doctor and he also observed Alex responding appropriately.

When I told Mom that Alex was waking up, it was the happiest she had been in a year. The doctors continually assessed his neurological condition. He progressed slowly. He could eventually answer questions with a thumbs-up and blinks. I asked Alex about his past, which tested his long-term memory. He remembered everything that I asked about. I then asked probing questions to assess his ability to think. Alex's mind was as sharp as ever. I played games with him in which he blinked to choose a move as I went through the possibilities. He would win more than he lost. Alex was all there, but his body had failed him.

On January 24, 2008, Alex was sent to a rehab hospital. He was one of three young men admitted on the same day. One had suffered a brain aneurysm, and the other suffered a gunshot wound to the head. This was difficult for me. I had never thought about young men being struck down this way. It is not possible to know the impact that these types of devastating injuries have on family members until you have experienced it. Our common wish was that rehab would lead to a good outcome. I then witnessed the suffering of family members when the doctors made the call to send the patient onward to long-term care. That crushed any hope that they had left. It felt like an impersonal and heartless process.

Mom insisted I give her daily updates while Alex was in rehab, so I called her every night at six to fill her in. We had high hopes that Alex would regain some control of his body. He could not swallow or talk, so they put a G-tube in his stomach to feed him with a liquid formula and to give him his numerous medications. He needed to be medicated hourly. Whenever the staff put Alex to bed, he was in intolerable pain. I asked him what hurt, and we went through a process where he identified that he was having radiating pain down his legs, originating from his lower back. I told the doctors what he had expressed. They sent him for an MRI of the lower back, but he could not lie still because of the pain. The doctor believed he had a compressed disk but decided that there was no viable treatment that could be used during his rehab. The physician instructed us to see an orthopedic surgeon after Alex was released. He left rehab on May 20, 2008. Alex had no fine-motor skills, could not talk, could not eat, and needed 24-hour care.

I remembered the time at Sharmar when I was 12 and had seen a 16-year-old girl with an anoxic brain injury. I talked over my feelings with Rose. We were resolved to never abandon Alex to an institution, so he came home. But the hospital made this decision even more complicated since the rehab team had dropped the ball on an important step. The medical staff was supposed to complete a safety check of our house before Alex's release. We found out about the safety check requirement on the day of his scheduled release. Our house was not safe at all. It was a tri-level with half of the garage renovated to accommodate a bedroom and bath. The bathroom was unsafe for a handicapped individual, and the bedroom was only 120 square feet. There was no ramp to the living area on the middle floor. Plus, the stairs up to the middle level were too steep to carry him up. We had to find a contractor who would build a ramp up to the living area and remodel the garage-level bathroom for handicapped accessibility. It would take three months to complete. The hospital sent Alex home, anyway.

In retrospect, I should have known that the hospital would release him without warning. The 24-year-old young man at the rehab who had had an aneurysm ran out of insurance. I learned the rehab hospital had called his mother the day the insurance terminated to let her know that he was being released and inquired, "Where should we drop your son off?" His mother had to leave work and drive the 30 miles to the hospital to talk with the doctor. A nursing home would not take him because he did not qualify for Medicaid and his insurance did not cover long-term care. The mother was forced to come up with $10,000 to keep him in the hospital for an additional week until she could prepare her home to accommodate him. The house was not even close to being appropriate for a person with his level of disability. The best that she could do was clear out the dining room and put in a hospital bed. He required 24-hour care and could not interact with anyone. There wasn't even a bathroom on the same floor. I wondered how she would be able to clean up a bowel movement or empty a leg bag. It struck me that this sort of horror story occurs all the time with families when the unthinkable happens to their loved ones. I never realized the secrets that lie behind the veil of medicine in the treatment of severely injured or incapacitated patients until Alex's struggles.

We brought Alex home and he had to endure the construction of the ramp and bathroom. Medicaid provided some help, but Rose and I were responsible for the bulk of his nursing care. It ended up taking four months to complete the construction. Alex could not lie flat on his back because of the spinal injury. In June, we met with an orthopedic surgeon and Alex had an MRI under sedation. There was a compressed disk in the L5-S1 lumbosacral joint of his lower back. The doctor ordered an electromyography study, and it concurred with the MRI. The first attempt at treatment was an injection of a steroid into his spine. He had several, but the treatments did not work. If he lay flat on his back, he was in such pain that he struggled and rolled out of bed. The doctor believed the only option was to do an anterior cervical discectomy and fusion.

Alex had the procedure in October 2008. During the recovery from surgery, they gave him morphine. The nurse looking after him was aloof. When Alex started showing signs of having aspirated, I hit the call button. Aspiration is a sign of having too much morphine. The nurse came in and looked at him. She gave him another dose of morphine by hitting a button on a dispensary device that fed into his IV. Alex was still having difficulty breathing, so I rang for help again and the nurse came in, but this time she was angry.

I told her, "He can't breathe."

She did not examine him and said, "Press the button on the morphine dispenser and give him another dose yourself."

I begged her to get a doctor, but she said no and walked off. Alex continued to get worse, and then he stopped breathing. I started CPR and yelled for the nurse at the top of my lungs. She came in, furious and ready to scold me, until she saw for herself how dire the circumstances were. She hit a code blue. It took seconds for medical staff to come into the room with a crash cart. They got Alex to cough after a few minutes.

The doctor ordered a bronchoscopy to look at the airway and concluded that he had aspirated. They took a sample of fluid and discovered that fluid contained the superbug MRSA (Methicillin-Resistant Staphylococcus Aureus). They sent Alex to the ICU and put him in an isolation chamber. There, a PICC (Inserted Central Catheter) was inserted in his neck. The PICC line was used to flow vancomycin into a large vein as a treatment for MRSA, because the doctors believed that the bacteria had reached his bloodstream.

They sent Alex home ten days later with an order to continue giving him massive doses of vancomycin for eight weeks through his PICC line. This ordeal had a significant impact on us as well as Mom. Alex's condition was far from secure. Mom prayed night and day for him. She lived in fear of Alex needing to go back to the hospital. Alex eventually recovered and had the PICC line removed.

For the next few years, Alex continued to have difficulties. He was in the ICU twice for pneumonia. Then he had two severe urinary tract infections that required hospitalizations. It seemed like every time Alex went to the hospital, Mom died a little. She had gone through so much in her life that having a grandchild continually fighting for his life was too much to handle, even with her fortitude.

Mom went through the five stages of grief over Alex. When the accident happened, she was in denial. Afterward, she became angry that this horrific thing had happened to her grandson. Then she tried to bargain with God to take her and cure Alex. Mom eventually became depressed. She wanted to be with Alex, but she was too sick to travel. Often, Mom would lament that she had lived too long and remembered how beautiful Heaven was.

Mom demanded frequent reports on Alex. I told her about how happy Alex was and how people loved to be around him. He was blessed with her disposition and strength. Mom finally accepted what had happened to her grandson. I think our talks were reassuring. My wife and I learned how to keep Alex in a sterile environment so that he would not catch pneumonia. We developed procedures to keep him safe from UTIs and other infections. He went five years without pneumonia or a UTI. We made sure that Alex interacted with people. This was our most effective medicine. He went to movies, and he loved to go to a zero-entry pool with his two friends Steve and Mary. The pool had a plastic wheelchair that Alex used to enter the shallow part. Steve and Mary stood him up and helped him balance. He was a favorite of the lifeguards and many of the patrons. Alex had inherited his grandfather's good looks and got frequent compliments from the young women at the pool. Alex took day trips to St. Louis and Kansas City to visit the museums, to the parks in the area, to the riverboat in Booneville to play poker (Alex inherited his grandfather's love of card games), and to concerts. Mom was always excited to hear about any of Alex's adventures.

Mom lived to see her granddaughter Natalia's wedding in June 2013. She could not travel, so we used Skype and a smartphone to transmit the ceremony to my sister's computer in Pueblo. Mom watched from her home. She cried during the wedding. Afterward, Natalia and her spouse drove to Colorado for their honeymoon and stopped in to visit Mom. Mom was walking on clouds.

Mom started feeling bad in April 2014. I thought that it was a cold. She had always bounced back from a cold in the past. But this time she did not improve. Mom kept getting worse. I talked to her often, and I had high hopes that she would recover. She was the most tenacious person I knew, and I thought nothing could ever keep her down. On the night of May 23, I heard an owl hooting outside of my bedroom window. It was annoying, and I tried to shut it up by going outside to scare it away. But it came back and started hooting again. I lay awake in bed remembering what happened the night an owl had hooted outside my mom's bedroom window in 1957. My grandfather had died. The next morning, I called Mom and she sounded weak, but we spoke for a while. Before I hung up, her last word to me was an out-of-place "Goodbye." I went to work, but that last word rang in my ears. Then I got a call from Ines telling me that Mom had died. There is no way to describe how I felt. I drove to Pueblo with my friend Bob and we attended her funeral. Mom's friends filled the church. As I gazed at everyone, I began to think that no one could really sum up her life, not even me or my sister. No individual could know all that Mom had been through. We had only an inkling of her character and depth of soul. I now look into the eyes of people and realize that there is more there than I or anyone else can see. Even though I spent most of my life around her, there is so much more I would like to learn. I never asked the questions when I had the chance. I wish I could meet some people whom she saved during the war. I want to know what kind of lives they led. How did Mom influence them?

GONE BUT NOT FORGOTTEN

Alex was so much like his grandmother. Even being severely disabled, people marveled at his resolve, his calm spirit, and cheerful disposition. He loved helping others. If he noticed that someone nearby was depressed, though he had no fine-motor control of his arms or legs, Alex would struggle to reach out and touch that person's arm. I was that person at times. This small but powerful gesture immediately cheered me up and gave me strength. Alex was extraordinary.

After Mom's death, we continued to care for Alex. We endeavored to keep him active and engaged. He went to physical therapy on a weekly basis to keep his tendons from atrophying. Alex had a great social life and made many friends. He was working on a communication computer with an eye-gaze system. With that computer, he could use his eyes to control it and it had software that allowed him to express his thoughts.

On May 26, 2020, Alex started having problems breathing. He registered a fever. I called the emergency room and talked to a nurse. She advised me to call an ambulance. They took him to the hospital. Normally, they did not allow family members to come in with patients because of COVID-19 protocols. But since Alex was nonverbal, they made an exception for me. They used a high-flow nasal cannula to stabilize his breathing. Then they did a swab for COVID-19. The medical staff believed he had it. We waited for two hours for his test to come back. In the meantime, the doctor thought he was working too hard to breathe and recommended that he be placed on a ventilator. I had seen Alex on a ventilator during six prior hospitalizations. Each time it was a horrendous experience, and I was hesitant. But they monitored his breathing and oxygen levels and finally convinced me it was necessary to save his life. We were still in the ER when the results of the COVID-19 test came back. It was negative. This result should not have comforted me because I did not know at the time that the PCR nasal swab test has false negative rates ranging from 1 to 30 percent. False negative results can occur for various reasons such as poor specimen collection techniques, testing too early in the infection, low viral load, or lab errors. The x-rays showed that Alex had pneumonia. They took him to the non-COVID-19 ICU. But they did not allow family members in the hospital because of the protocols. So, they sent me home. I can't imagine what it was like for Alex to be so sick and not have family beside him as he suffered.

The doctors tried every possible antibiotic combination, but nothing worked. The infection spread to his chest cavity. They cultured the fluid in his lungs and chest cavity, but the bacteria would not grow. They could not identify what was responsible for the infection. He lost so much of his lung capacity that after two weeks he was sent home and placed in hospice care.

I did not have an inkling of what Mom had gone through in watching people die of TB when she was in quarantine or when she sat with patients during their last moments in the nursing home or when she sat with my father as he took his last breath. Until now. Sitting with my son as life slowly drained from him still haunts me every day. Many of my friends in the medical profession believe that Alex had an undiagnosed case of COVID-19. Given my experiences during Alex's hospital stays, I tend to agree with them.

During Alex's time in hospice care, Rose and I reminisced with him about Australia, where we had lived when I was a Fulbright Fellow in 1992. Even though he was only four years old at the time, he nodded that he remembered. I asked him if he wanted me to read what I had written for this book about his grandma. He did. So, I read what I had completed. And he listened intently. After I finished, he wanted me to continue reading. I told him it was not done yet, but I summarized in my own words what else I would write about. He smiled and touched me. I promised him that I would finish the book. He let me know that he approved enthusiastically.

Alex was given morphine for comfort, but it did little in the last few hours as he gasped for air. I asked him if he saw Grandma in a meadow waving at him and he nodded yes.

Alex passed away on June 11 at 2:39 a.m. Since his passing, I feel like there is a large hole in the middle of my soul that I continually fall into and struggle to pull myself out of. It only takes a memory to push me back in. The mental anguish is unbearable at times. Occasionally, my mind plays tricks and I think I can hear him. I am told that people who suffer the loss of a child have similar experiences that stay with them for the rest of their lives.

Alex had lived with us for 12 and a half years before his death. I am so glad that he was part of our lives for those years. It enriched us. After he died, there was an unprecedented outpouring of sympathy from the hundreds of people whose lives he had affected through his courage, personality, caring, and kindness. I take comfort that some part of him lives on through us and, in turn, through the people whose lives we impact. I miss him every day.

Epilogue

The war always haunted Mom. I wish I could have eased her pain. There were times I prayed that World War II had never happened and that my father and mother could have lived normal lives. But I also understood that my existence was directly connected to every tragic experience that they had endured.

My family paid a steep price for the nationalistic fervor and extremism that had occurred during the 20th century. So many other families suffered much more. My mom's first thoughts once the fighting ended in Germany were about the well-being of family and friends—she was obsessed with finding people. Mom tried to learn what had happened to her relatives in Leipzig. But following years of searching, she could not find out. By the time Mom arrived in the United States, she had lost all hope that they had survived. When I asked about them as a child, it triggered memories that she tried to suppress and she would say as little as possible. Eventually, I stopped asking. I regret not finding out their names. With the available tools on the internet, I could have found some closure by searching through databases.

When I was 14, I had asked Dad a question while doing research for a class assignment: "How could people in a civilized country like Germany allow Hitler to come into power?" I was always impressed by my father's "street smarts" which he had learned as a runaway. His views were always simple and clear. My dad reminded me about Frenchie and the carny. "How did Frenchie allow his money to be taken so easily by a con artist?"

When I was seven years old, Frenchie took me to a carnival. He bought me tickets for the kiddie rides. After I used them all, we were walking toward his truck when a carnival barker at a booth caught Frenchie's attention. He was playing some sort of numbers game. The man convinced Frenchie to buy one chance. Even though neither of us could understand the rules of the game, Frenchie won a small trinket, which he gave to me. Then the carny said that since Frenchie had won one game, the prize would be bigger in the next play. He continued to reel Frenchie into his web, yet neither of us understood the rules. The grand prize was a rifle that Frenchie coveted. So, the carny kept stringing Frenchie along, making him think he was close to winning. Finally, Frenchie had spent every bit of the $300 in his wallet. The carny promised that if Frenchie left to get more money, his place on the board would be saved. Frenchie drove me back home. I told Dad what was happening. Before Frenchie could depart to find more money, Dad tried to stop him. But Frenchie didn't listen. He went back to his house and raided the family emergency funds. He lost it all and never got the rifle. Frenchie was too embarrassed to tell us how much. I remember that a month later I saw the same kind of rifle at the Army and Navy surplus store for $150.

Dad told me that there were a lot of people in the world like the carny. He called this type of person a *prevarant*, which means grifter in Croatian. Grifters have some mixture of psychopathy, narcissism, and an ability to persuade people to do things that are against their nature and best interest. Con artists understand human psychology. They have perfected the manipulation of core emotions such as anger, fear, sadness, disgust, surprise, anticipation, trust, and joy. The strongest of these is fear, and that is what cons depend upon the most. They are highly skilled at reading people, have a total lack of conscience, and are chameleons because of their ability to adjust their looks or image based on the intended deception. Grifters know how to blind even the most intelligent person to the truth. They can strip someone of common sense and moral compass.

A grifter can even deceive a streetwise person like my father. Dad muttered the names of Tony Sraka and Dimitri. I finally understood why Frenchie behaved so foolishly. He became so immersed in the con that he didn't realize it, even though it was obvious to others around him.

Dad grimly looked at me. "A grifter is usually satisfied by taking something of value from you. But there is always one who desires much more, including your soul; and with the right opportunity, it is possible to even take that. Why did it happen? Those who could have stopped Hitler made the wrong choices." He paused in thought. "So many died in the madness that followed." It was a time of madmen. And memories fade. And lessons learned are forgotten.

ABOUT THE AUTHOR

Although this is the first memoir written by Dr. Mark A. Prelas, he is an award-winning author. His works include numerous books, articles and editorials in the field of science, nonproliferation, energy, the environment and counterterrorism.

Mark is a professor emeritus in the college of engineering at the University of Missouri where he began his career in teaching, research and service in 1979.

Dear Reader,

If you have enjoyed reading my book,
please do leave a review on Amazon or Goodreads.
A few kind words would be enough.
This would be greatly appreciated.

Alternatively, if you have read my book as Kindle eBook you could
leave a rating.
That is just one simple click, indicating how many stars of five you
think this book deserves.
This will only cost you a split second.
Thank you very much in advance!

Mark A. Prelas

PHOTOS

Josip in Split, circa 1926

Jure with brothers, 1924

Katicà Bek as a teenager, circa 1937

Katicà and Jure's Civil Wedding, 1943

Yelca and Jako, 1946

The Bek family in Popovaca, circa 1946

Jure in Lübeck, circa 1947

*Ines and a friend watching Santa from a window, Christmas, circa
1947*

Second wedding of Katicà and Jure, 1947

Yelca's funeral, 1947

Katicà and Jure's Wedding Reception, 1947

Katicà with Ines, circa 1947-1948

Inga with Ines, Lübeck, 1948

Father Kordis (left), Katicà, Ines and Jure, circa 1948

Jure and Ines, Pueblo, Colorado, February 1951

Uncle Mike and Aunt Mary and Author as baby, circa 1954

From left to right: Author, Jure, Ines and Katicà, 1958

Alex at age 15 in 2001

Alex at 26 in 2013

AMSTERDAM PUBLISHERS HOLOCAUST LIBRARY

The series **Holocaust Survivor Memoirs World War II** consists of the following autobiographies of survivors:

Outcry. Holocaust Memoirs, by Manny Steinberg

Hank Brodt Holocaust Memoirs. A Candle and a Promise, by Deborah Donnelly

The Dead Years. Holocaust Memoirs, by Joseph Schupack

Rescued from the Ashes. The Diary of Leokadia Schmidt, Survivor of the Warsaw Ghetto, by Leokadia Schmidt

My Lvov. Holocaust Memoir of a twelve-year-old Girl, by Janina Hescheles

Remembering Ravensbrück. From Holocaust to Healing, by Natalie Hess

Wolf. A Story of Hate, by Zeev Scheinwald with Ella Scheinwald

Save my Children. An Astonishing Tale of Survival and its Unlikely Hero, by Leon Kleiner with Edwin Stepp

Holocaust Memoirs of a Bergen-Belsen Survivor & Classmate of Anne Frank, by Nanette Blitz Konig

Defiant German - Defiant Jew. A Holocaust Memoir from inside the Third Reich, by Walter Leopold with Les Leopold

In a Land of Forest and Darkness. The Holocaust Story of two Jewish Partisans, by Sara Lustigman Omelinski

Holocaust Memories. Annihilation and Survival in Slovakia, by Paul Davidovits

From Auschwitz with Love. The Inspiring Memoir of Two Sisters' Survival, Devotion and Triumph Told by Manci Grunberger Beran & Ruth Grunberger Mermelstein, by Daniel Seymour

Remetz. Resistance Fighter and Survivor of the Warsaw Ghetto, by Jan Yohay Remetz

My March Through Hell. A Young Girl's Terrifying Journey to Survival, by Halina Kleiner with Edwin Stepp

———

The series **Holocaust Survivor True Stories WWII** consists of the following biographies:

Among the Reeds. The true story of how a family survived the Holocaust, by Tammy Bottner

A Holocaust Memoir of Love & Resilience. Mama's Survival from Lithuania to America, by Ettie Zilber

Living among the Dead. My Grandmother's Holocaust Survival Story of Love and Strength, by Adena Bernstein Astrowsky

Heart Songs. A Holocaust Memoir, by Barbara Gilford

Shoes of the Shoah. The Tomorrow of Yesterday, by Dorothy Pierce

Hidden in Berlin. A Holocaust Memoir, by Evelyn Joseph Grossman

Separated Together. The Incredible True WWII Story of Soulmates Stranded an Ocean Apart, by Kenneth P. Price, Ph.D.

The Man Across the River. The incredible story of one man's will to survive the Holocaust, by Zvi Wiesenfeld

If Anyone Calls, Tell Them I Died. A Memoir, by Emanuel (Manu) Rosen

The House on Thrömerstrasse. A Story of Rebirth and Renewal in the Wake of the Holocaust, by Ron Vincent

Dancing with my Father. His hidden past. Her quest for truth. How Nazi Vienna shaped a family's identity, by Jo Sorochinsky

The Story Keeper. Weaving the Threads of Time and Memory - A Memoir, by Fred Feldman

Krisia's Silence. The Girl who was not on Schindler's List, by Ronny Hein

Defying Death on the Danube. A Holocaust Survival Story, by Debbie J. Callahan with Henry Stern

A Doorway to Heroism. A decorated German-Jewish Soldier who became an American Hero, by Rabbi W. Jack Romberg

The Shoemaker's Son. The Life of a Holocaust Resister, by Laura Beth Bakst

The Redhead of Auschwitz. A True Story, by Nechama Birnbaum

Land of Many Bridges. My Father's Story, by Bela Ruth Samuel Tenenholtz

Creating Beauty from the Abyss. The Amazing Story of Sam Herciger, Auschwitz Survivor and Artist, by Lesley Ann Richardson

On Sunny Days We Sang. A Holocaust Story of Survival and Resilience, by Jeannette Grunhaus de Gelman

Painful Joy. A Holocaust Family Memoir, by Max J. Friedman

I Give You My Heart. A True Story of Courage and Survival, by Wendy Holden

In the Time of Madmen, by Mark A. Prelas

Monsters and Miracles. Horror, Heroes and the Holocaust, by Ira Wesley Kitmacher

Flower of Vlora. Growing up Jewish in Communist Albania, by Anna Kohen

Zaidy's War, by Martin Bodek

––––––

The series **Jewish Children in the Holocaust** consists of the following autobiographies of Jewish children hidden during WWII in the Netherlands:

Searching for Home. The Impact of WWII on a Hidden Child, by Joseph Gosler

See You Tonight and Promise to be a Good Boy! War memories, by Salo Muller

Sounds from Silence. Reflections of a Child Holocaust Survivor, Psychiatrist and Teacher, by Robert Krell

Sabine's Odyssey. A Hidden Child and her Dutch Rescuers, by Agnes Schipper

The Journey of a Hidden Child, by Harry Pila with Robin Black

––––––

The series **New Jewish Fiction** consists of the following novels, written by Jewish authors. All novels are set in the time during or after the Holocaust.

The Corset Maker. A Novel, by Annette Libeskind Berkovits

Escaping the Whale. The Holocaust is over. But is it ever over for the next generation? by Ruth Rotkowitz

When the Music Stopped. Willy Rosen's Holocaust, by Casey Hayes

Hands of Gold. One Man's Quest to Find the Silver Lining in Misfortune, by Roni Robbins

There was a garden in Nuremberg. A Novel, by Navina Michal Clemerson

Aftermath: Coming-of-Age on Three Continents, by Annette Libeskind Berkovits

The Girl Who Counted Numbers. A Novel, by Roslyn Bernstein

The Butterfly and the Axe, by Omer Bartov

––––––––––––––

The series **Holocaust Books for Young Adults** consists of the following novels, based on true stories:

The Boy behind the Door. How Salomon Kool Escaped the Nazis, by David Tabatsky

Running for Shelter. A True Story, by Suzette Sheft

The Precious Few. An Inspirational Saga of Courage based on True Stories, by David Twain with Art Twain

Want to be an AP book reviewer?

Reviews are very important in a world dominated by the social media and social proof. Please drop us a line if you want to join the *AP review team*. We will then add you to our list of advance reviewers. No strings attached, and we promise that we will not be spamming you.

info@amsterdampublishers.com